Trade Show In A Day

Get it done right, get it done fast™

The Planning Shop

with Rhonda Abrams
and Betsy Bozdech

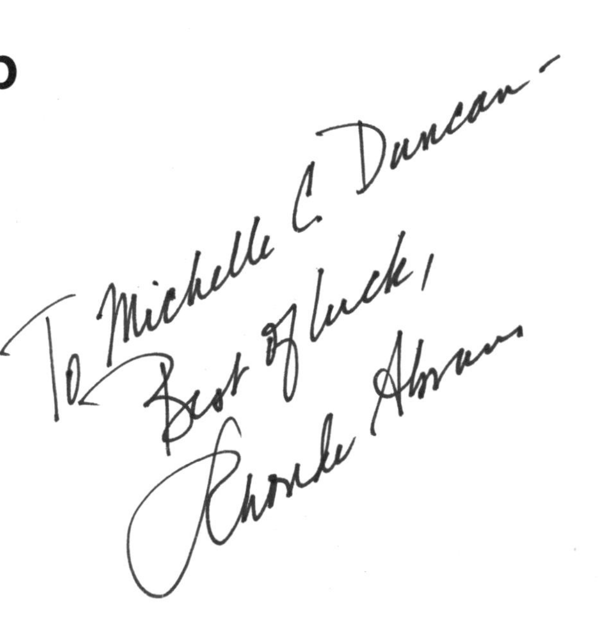

thePlanningshop

PALO ALTO, CALIFORNIA

Trade Show In A Day: Get it done right, get it done fast!™
©2006 by Rhonda Abrams. Published by The Planning Shop™

ISBN 13: 978-0-9740801-7-8
ISBN: 0-9740801-7-9
PCN: 2006930280

Managing Editor: Maggie Canon
Project Editor: Mireille Majoor
Cover and interior design: Diana Van Winkle, Arthur Wait

Services for our readers

Colleges, business schools, corporate purchasing:
The Planning Shop offers special discounts and supplemental materials for universities, business schools, and corporate training. Contact:

info@PlanningShop.com
or call 650-289-9120

Free business tips and information:
To receive The Planning Shop's free email newsletter on starting and growing a successful business, sign up at: www.PlanningShop.com.

The Planning Shop™
555 Bryant Street, #180
Palo Alto, CA 94301 USA
650-289-9120

Fax: 650-289-9125
Email: info@PlanningShop.com
www.PlanningShop.com

The Planning Shop™ is a division of Rhonda, Inc., a California corporation.

"This publication is designed to provide accurate and authoritative information in regard to the subject matter covered. It is sold with the understanding that the publisher and author are not engaged in rendering legal, accounting, or other professional services. If legal advice or other expert assistance is required, seek the services of a competent professional."

—*from a Declaration of Principles, jointly adopted by a committee of the American Bar Association and a committee of publishers*

Printed in Canada

10 9 8 7 6 5 4 3 2 1

About
The Planning Shop

The Planning Shop specializes in creating business resources for entrepreneurs. The Planning Shop's books and other products are based on years of real-world experience, and they share secrets and strategies from entrepreneurs, CEOs, investors, lenders, and seasoned business experts. Entrepreneurs have used The Planning Shop's products to launch, run, and expand businesses in every industry.

CEO Rhonda Abrams founded The Planning Shop in 1999. An experienced entrepreneur, Rhonda has started three successful companies. Her background gives her a real-life understanding of the challenges facing people who set up and run their own businesses. The author of numerous books on entrepreneurship, Rhonda has had three books appear on Bookscan's Top 50 Business Bestseller list. Her first book, *The Successful Business Plan: Secrets & Strategies,* has sold over 600,000 copies and was acclaimed by *Forbes* and *Inc.* magazines as one of the top ten business books for entrepreneurs. Rhonda also writes the nation's most widely circulated column on entrepreneurship and small business. Successful Business Strategies appears on USAToday.com and Inc.com and in more than one hundred newspapers, reaching millions of readers each week.

The Planning Shop's books have been adopted at more than four hundred business schools, colleges, and universities.

The Planning Shop's expanding line of business books includes:

- The **Successful Business series**, assisting entrepreneurs and business students in planning and growing businesses. Titles include *Six-Week Start-Up*, *What Business Should I Start?*, and *The Owner's Manual for Small Business.*
- The **In A Day series**, enabling entrepreneurs to tackle a critical business task and "Get it done right, get it done fast.™" Titles include *Business Plan In A Day*, *Winning Presentation In A Day*, and *Finding an Angel Investor In A Day*.
- The **Better Business Bureau series**, helping entrepreneurs and consumers successfully make serious financial decisions. Titles include *Buying a Franchise*, *Buying a Home*, and *Starting an eBay Business.*

At The Planning Shop, now and in the future, you'll find a range of business resources. Learn more at: www.PlanningShop.com.

The *In A Day* Promise

Get it done right, get it done fast

You're busy. We can help.

The Planning Shop is dedicated to helping entrepreneurs create and grow successful businesses. As entrepreneurs ourselves, we understand the many demands placed on you. We don't assume that you're a dummy, just that you're short on time.

This *In A Day* book will enable you to complete a critical business task in a hurry—and in the right way. You'll get it done right and get it done fast.

Can you learn what you need to know in just twenty-four hours? Yes. Perhaps the twenty-four hours won't be consecutive. You may start—pause for an hour, day, or week to take care of other business—then return to the task later. Or, you may have some research or other preparation to do before you can complete this project.

We'll guide you through the process, show you what you absolutely have to do, and give you tips and tricks to help you reach your goals. We've talked to the experts and done the research so you don't have to. We've also eliminated any unnecessary steps so you don't waste your valuable time. That's the *In A Day* promise.

When you have a business task you need to do *now*, The Planning Shop's *In A Day* books will help you get it done—in as little as a day.

Need to Plan a Trade Show Fast?
This Book Is For You!

Are you about to exhibit at a trade show? Overwhelmed with all the details? Want to make sure that people come to your booth? And then know how to turn them into customers once they stop by?

If you want to make the most of your trade show investment—and easily handle all the logistics of managing a trade show exhibit—this book is for you!

At some point, almost every business exhibits its products or services at a trade show—whether it's at a major exposition in a huge convention center, an industry conference in a hotel ballroom, or even a mixer at the local Chamber of Commerce. If you're ready to take on the world of trade shows, this book will help you succeed.

Trade shows are a multibillion-dollar industry for a reason: They work. They bring interested buyers together with interested sellers. In just a few short days—sometimes even hours—you can present your products or services to more potential clients or customers than you might in a year's worth of sales calls.

Trade Show In A Day was created for busy people like you. This guide provides you with the critical information you need to select the right show, manage all the details, and get the most out of the time and money you put in—all in record time!

Trade Show In A Day includes helpful tools for planning each show you attend, including:

- Trade show timeline: what to do and when to do it
- How to find and select the right show
- Selecting and designing your booth
- Trade show services: which ones you really need and which you don't
- Budgeting worksheets
- Detailed logistics planning, including shipping
- Sample scripts for talking to people who visit your booth
- Post-show follow-up to turn browsers into buyers

Trade Show In A Day gives you everything you need to plan and execute a successful trade show. And it helps you *get it done right—and get it done fast!*

How to Use This Book

To create *Trade Show In A Day*, we gathered the most useful and critical information from people who organize and attend trade shows for a living. We focused on what you need to know to make your trade show experience a complete success.

Trade Show In A Day is organized in a step-by-step fashion, outlining the keys to effective trade show preparation, attendance, and follow-up.

If you're brand-new to trade shows, you'll want to follow this book from start to finish.

If you've exhibited at trade shows before but want to make your trade show experience more successful, go straight to the sections of most interest to you.

Within each step, you'll find the tools you need to help you make the most of your trade show experience, including:

- QuickTips giving insiders' secrets and strategies to make your show a success
- A Trade Show Timeline, explaining exactly what to do—and when to do it
- Checklists of what to take, what to order, who to contact, how to follow up, and more
- Worksheets to help you plan and stay organized
- Sample scripts showing you exactly how to communicate with customers before, during, and after the show

Generally, the steps follow the natural progression of trade show planning:

Choosing the show. How to find and book the right show for your business. Which show services you need—and which you don't.

Marketing. Pre-show promotions that drive attendees to your booth. Which marketing materials to take and which to leave at the office. Making the most of giveaways.

Your time at the show. Attracting attendees, effectively approaching and talking to attendees, qualifying leads. Making the most of your time outside the booth. Even what to wear!

Follow-up. Turning leads into actual sales. When to contact them, what to send, what to say.

Your booth. When you need a professionally prepared booth, what kind to use, and where to get it.

Critical logistics. How to ship your booth and materials. What to take. And which critical materials you should *never* ship!

Trade Show In A Day is your one-stop resource for getting the most out of trade shows, conferences, and exhibits of every size. Get it done right, get it done fast!

How to Use This Book

Throughout this book you'll see worksheets and checklists you can use to do your own trade show planning and evaluation. Two examples are shown at right. If there's not enough space on the sheets, use a separate piece of paper to record your thoughts and data.

Trade Show Goals

Use this worksheet to list potential trade show goals for your business.

What is your primary trade show goal?

What is your secondary trade show goal?

What are your other trade show goals?

Checklist: Shipping to the Show

Use this checklist to keep track of everything you'll be taking to the show.

SHIP AHEAD OF TIME:

Booth/exhibit materials

- ☐ Booth
- ☐ Banners and signs
- ☐ Product display holders
- ☐ Lights
- ☐ Photos and illustrations
- ☐ Computers and audiovisual equipment

Products/Product Samples

- ☐ New products
- ☐ Existing products
- ☐ Past projects binder

Marketing Materials

- ☐ Catalogs
- ☐ Order forms
- ☐ Brochures
- ☐ Sales sheets
- ☐ Business cards
- ☐ Giveaways
- ☐ Other:

Booth Supplies

- ☐ Lead forms or trade show notebooks
- ☐ Pens
- ☐ Stapler
- ☐ String
- ☐ Packing tape
- ☐ Permanent marker
- ☐ Shipping labels
- ☐ Shipping envelopes/ materials and paperwork
- ☐ A pad of plain notepaper
- ☐ An appointment book/ calendar for making follow-up appointments
- ☐ Order forms
- ☐ Other:

Other Useful Items

- ☐ Antibacterial hand sanitizer
- ☐ Wet wipes
- ☐ Spray cleaner and paper towels
- ☐ Hand vacuum
- ☐ Duct tape
- ☐ Scissors
- ☐ Universal screwdriver
- ☐ Pliers
- ☐ Box cutter
- ☐ 3-to-2-prong plug converter
- ☐ Extra lightbulbs
- ☐ Batteries
- ☐ Extension cords
- ☐ Power strip
- ☐ Flashlight
- ☐ Plastic bags with zip closures
- ☐ Other:

Personal Items

- ☐ Bottled water
- ☐ Dry snacks
- ☐ Breath mints
- ☐ Small first aid kit

TAKE WITH YOU:

- ☐ Show paperwork
- ☐ Electronic copies of marketing materials
- ☐ Hard copies of marketing materials
- ☐ Extra business cards
- ☐ Extra pen(s)
- ☐ Keys (for opening boxes)
- ☐ A list of emergency contact information
- ☐ Extra lead forms or trade show notebooks

Trade Show In A Day
Contents

1

STEP 1: Choose the Right Show

Accomplishments

In this step you'll:

- ☐ 1. Learn about types of trade shows and other exhibit opportunities
- ☐ 2. Find out why attendees typically go to trade shows
- ☐ 3. Find out why businesses typically exhibit at trade shows
- ☐ 4. Learn where to find out about potential shows and conferences
- ☐ 5. Learn how to identify your target customer
- ☐ 6. Learn where to find potential targets

Time-Saving Tools

You'll complete this step more quickly if you have the following handy:

- ☐ 1. Your contact list or database
- ☐ 2. A list of associations serving your industry
- ☐ 3. Information about your target customers or clients

Step 1: Choose the Right Show

Trade shows build businesses. In just a few short days you'll reach a large number of industry contacts, potential suppliers, and most important, buyers!

Not only are all these key prospects under one roof, they're eager to see what you have to offer. Trade show attendees have an interest and a need—and have set aside the time—to look at your products or services and to get to know you and your company.

At the right trade show, with the right approach, you can:

- Land that big customer
- Launch a new product
- Develop a mailing list of hot leads
- Find a key strategic partner to reach a larger market
- Enhance relationships with your existing customers

Exhibiting at a trade show can be one of the best business decisions you'll ever make. If you choose the right show, it's an efficient and effective way to build your business.

To find the right trade show for you, you need to know:

- The different types of trade shows
- What your goals are
- How to find out about potential shows
- Who your target market is

QUICK**TIP**

You're at the right show when ...

... you reach the right customers or prospects and they're eager to do business. So before you book a show, find out what kind of people actually attend the trade show you're considering. Get a list of past exhibitors, either from trade show management or from trade show websites, call a few of them, and ask about the nature and number of attendees at previous years' shows.

QUICK**TIP**

Look Before You Leap

The best way to find out whether a trade show is a good fit for you and your business is to go as an attendee. You'll see who attends, who exhibits there (including your competitors and partners), and what the latest industry trends are. Finding out in advance if a show is a good fit for your business saves time and money.

Take advantage of having so many industry contacts in one place. Set meetings with potential customers or offer to take them out for a meal. If you're not tied to an exhibit, your schedule will be more flexible.

1. Types of Shows

The type of trade show you choose to attend affects virtually every other decision you make while preparing for it. Even if your business sells only one product or service, the most effective sales venue for it will vary, depending on what you're selling and who you're selling it to.

Let's say your company makes gourmet salsa. If your goal is to sell the salsa directly to as many new customers as possible, your best bet is to exhibit at a broad food show with thousands of attendees and hundreds of exhibitors, like the annual International Fancy Food and Confection Show. But if you want to position your salsa as a leader in the Hispanic food market, a smaller, more targeted conference might be a better choice—one like the Expo Comida Latina.

Ultimately, the right type of show for *your* business depends on your goals and your target market. So before you can choose a show, you need to know your options.

Most non-consumer exhibition opportunities fall into one of two broad categories: trade shows (also called expositions, or "expos") and conferences. At a trade show or expo, the primary action takes place on the exhibit hall floor. Attendees are there to visit booths, and all non-exhibit activities are secondary. At a conference, the opposite is true. Attendees are there to go to seminars and educational sessions, visiting the exhibition hall only during breaks in their daily schedules.

	TRADE SHOW/EXPOSITION	CONFERENCE
Primary goal	To bring industry professionals together and to introduce new or existing products and services and/or new or existing vendors.	To gather industry or association professionals together for educational or policy-setting purposes.
Who attends?	Buyers and decision makers. Anyone involved in the industry.	Anyone in an industry or association who is interested in, requires continuing education in, or has a say in the future of the industry. Conferences also provide excellent opportunities for networking
Where held?	Depends on size. Often held in large convention centers or major hotels and frequently in destination cities (Las Vegas, Chicago, San Francisco).	Depends on size. Often held in mid-size convention centers or hotels. Can be in destination or smaller cities (San Diego, Tuscon).
When held?	Year-round.	Year-round.
How long?	Average three days. Show floor is open for the duration of the event.	Average three days. Show floor is open only at specific times during the event.
Examples	BookExpo America (BEA), International Pool & Spa Expo, National Industrial Fastener Show, Corporate & Channel Computing Expo (C3).	American Academy of Pediatrics National Conference & Exhibition, International Chain Salon Association Conference.

QUICK**TIP**

Tableton Shows

Many smaller associations and niche industries have exhibit opportunities at their conferences and seminars. In most cases, displays are restricted to what an exhibitor can fit on top of a single table. These "tabletop shows" are great for small businesses with limited resources: there's no expensive booth to buy and attendees are usually highly qualified.

These two larger categories of trade shows and conferences have several important subcategories:

- **National.** National shows and conferences bring together industry professionals from across the country (and sometimes from around the world). Attendees are often higher-level decision makers than those at regional shows. These shows also have more attendees and exhibitors than their regional counterparts and tend to have larger, more elaborate booths and displays.

- **Regional.** Regional shows and conferences allow subsets of an industry to meet and address issues of particular concern to their segment of the industry. Attendees are often lower-level decision makers than those at national shows. These shows are generally smaller in size and tend to have smaller booths and displays. A regional show is a great starter show for a first-time exhibitor.

- **Horizontal (industry-specific).** Horizontal shows bring together a wide range of sellers within a common industry—for example, the sporting goods industry. Attendees may be interested in all of the exhibits (if they're general sporting goods retailers) or only a certain subset (if they're surf shop owners).

- **Vertical (market-specific).** Vertical shows and conferences bring together vendors and customers who are interested in a narrowly focused market segment. Exhibitors choose these shows because they have products or services that appeal to a niche market. Attendees choose them because they know they will find the products and services that interest them.

Is Bigger Better?

When it comes to trade shows and conferences, bigger is not necessarily better. Large and small shows each have advantages and disadvantages. While it may not be a make-or-break factor, consider size when choosing which shows to attend.

	PROS	CONS
Small shows	• Logistics are usually more manageable (particularly helpful for someone planning their first show). • Tend to be less expensive. • You're less likely to be overshadowed by bigger exhibitors. • You can often use a simple tabletop exhibit—no booth required. • Attendees are typically from specific niche markets.	• Fewer attendees mean fewer potential leads, particularly if you discover it's not the right show for you after you get there. • Attendees are less likely to have high-level buying power. • Show management can be less organized than at big shows. • Fewer resources for exhibitors. • May attract little attention within the industry/trade press.
Large shows	• Numerous attendees mean lots of potential leads—if you can get them to your booth. • Exhibiting next to big companies' booths can sometimes drive more traffic your way. • Higher-level decision makers are more likely to attend. • Show management is used to juggling a lot of demands and is more likely to have readily available resources for exhibitors. • Greater visibility within the industry, which can be helpful if you're launching a new product or brand.	• Logistics and costs can be overwhelming. • If you're a small exhibitor, you might disappear among large companies' expensive booths. • You're more likely to look amateurish if you don't have a sophisticated booth. • Higher risk of being tucked away in a low-traffic zone. • When thousands of people attend, it's harder to target only the ones you want to meet.

Creative Alternatives

Trade shows and conferences aren't the only options when it comes to exhibiting your products and services. Consider these alternatives as well. Each can complement an exhibit hall presence or, in some cases, substitute for it:

- **Chamber of Commerce mixer.** Many local chambers have regular events for member businesses. Call yours to find out if you can set up a table at the next one. Take a sign or banner, some business cards, and brochures or product information sheets. These mixers are excellent for raising awareness for your product or service. And they're also great networking opportunities.
- **Association meeting.** Some associations have exhibit areas at their regular meetings (though not always and not often in the case of local branches). But call and ask. They may give you an opportunity to display.
- **Client/customer seminar.** Bring clients and customers to you! Plan a training session or informational seminar at your office (or if that's not feasible, in a small hotel meeting room). Invite local customers to attend.
- **Open house.** If a big trade show or conference is coming to your city, but you can't afford (or don't want) to exhibit, invite key prospects to visit your offices instead. This is an especially good idea if you're located near the conference. They may welcome a break and you'll get to roll out the red carpet.
- **Hospitality event.** Rather than pay for exhibit hall space, some companies invest their trade show budget in a hotel suite. If you set up a hospitality area, you can invite prospective customers to come by for drinks or a meal.

Get your product or service in front of the people who matter! When it comes to exhibiting, the only limitation is your imagination.

Trade Show History 101

The concept of trade shows dates back to the medieval marketplace, where merchants would sell their wares from stalls in the center of town. Some markets served specific trades or guilds, acting like modern trade shows. Others sold goods directly to passersby, foreshadowing consumer and public shows.

2. Attendees' show goals

Attendees go to shows and conferences for as many reasons as exhibitors choose to rent exhibit space. However, the *key* reason usually boils down to one of the main objectives listed below. Understanding attendees' motivations helps you set your own goals. Making the match between your needs and theirs is key to your success.

Key attendee objectives include:

- **Getting exposure to new products and services.** Many attendees go to trade shows with a specific business need to address or problem to solve. They're hoping to find a fresh solution on the show floor. As an exhibitor, your job is to display your latest products or services, then discover the attendee's problem or need and convince them that your solution is the best one.
- **Gathering specific product/service information.** Statistics show that up to three-quarters of trade show attendees have an agenda when they arrive at a trade show. Many come with a list of companies to visit, planning to collect specific information about products and services. Attendees with this goal may request catalogs or other information to take home.
- **Purchasing products or services.** At some shows, attendees want to place orders. Be prepared. Take everything you need to process those orders, whether that means paper forms or a credit card processing system.
- **Keeping up on industry trends and innovations.** One of the most efficient ways for attendees to find out what's new and exciting in their industry is to tour the exhibit floor. Even a quick circuit yields insights into what's new and improved.

QUICK**TIP**

Validation, Please!

It's nice to know you've made a good decision. Many attendees come to trade shows to confirm choices they've already made—to make sure their current suppliers are the best ones or that they're getting the best deal possible on the best product. Leave plenty of room in your show schedule for current customers, so you can provide them with that reassurance.

- **Making industry contacts.** Whether an attendee is looking for a new strategic partner, a new supplier, or a new job, going to a trade show is an efficient way to do it. Trade shows provide attendees with a broad pool of new contacts under one roof.
- **Education.** Traveling to a show or conference can be expensive. Many attendees justify the cost by calling it continuing education in their industry. That's why most trade shows and expos offer at least a few seminars or sessions in addition to an exhibit hall.

3. Exhibitors' show goals

One of the best ways to ensure that you get the most out of attending a trade show is to establish clear, realistic goals beforehand. "Realistic" is the key word here: If you have a small booth at a three-day show with 5,000 attendees, for instance, you can't expect to talk to all of them. Once you've decided on your primary goal, tailor the rest of your exhibit experience to meeting it, from choosing which show to attend to planning marketing materials to designing your display graphics.

The most common exhibitor trade show goals include:

- **Gathering sales leads.** This is the number 1 reason that companies attend trade shows. The best way to meet prospective new customers (or "leads") is to talk to as many attendees as possible. You won't have time to connect with everyone, and not everyone will be interested in talking to you. Figure out how long you need to spend with a person to determine whether they're a good prospect or "qualified lead" (usually it's just a few minutes). Then do your own math to set a realistic goal for the number of potential leads you can gain at a given show.
- **Meeting other people in the industry.** New customers are your prime targets, but don't forget the importance of making industry contacts. The company across the aisle could be the perfect strategic partner. Take time to walk the show floor when traffic is slow and chat with anyone whose product, service, or booth intrigues you.
- **Reinforcing existing relationships**. How often do you have the chance to talk to your current customers or industry contacts face to face? Trade shows are great opportunities for catching up with business colleagues. If you want them to *keep* doing business with you, make time for them during the show.
- **Launching a new product or marketing message**. There's a reason why Apple announces their latest gizmos at the yearly Macworld show. With all of those Mac lovers—and reporters!—gathered in one spot, the battle to get their attention is half won before a single word is spoken. Trade shows are magnets for industry press and decision makers. If you have something important to say, why not say it where you know people will listen?

- **Raising company visibility**. Sometimes the best reason to go to a trade show is that people in the industry will notice if you're *not* there. This goal rarely affects the bottom line directly, but there are times when you have to keep up with the Joneses. But be sure to think carefully before exhibiting for this reason alone.
- **Seeing what the competition is up to**. Opportunities to scope out the competition "up close and personal" are usually few and far between. On the show floor, however, your biggest competitor might be right around the corner. This will give you the chance to learn more about their newest products and sales strategies, among other things. But remember: They're probably looking at you, too.
- **Learning more about the industry**. Attendees aren't the only ones who see trade shows as a great chance to brush up their industry skills and knowledge. If your business is new, spending a weekend on the show floor and attending a seminar or two provides the perfect crash course. If your company is already established, you'll benefit by staying up-to-date.

ROI vs. ROO

Many companies go to a trade show with the goal of achieving a specific, quantifiable Return On Investment (or ROI). The easiest way to calculate a show's ROI is to add up the amount of business brought in by each lead generated at the show and then divide it by the total show budget. For example, if you met 10 good leads at the show who each brought in $10,000 in new business and you spent $5,000 on show costs, your ROI would be 10 x 10,000 ÷ 5,000 = 20 times the amount of your initial investment.

The problem with trade show ROIs is that they can be difficult to calculate precisely. It's often hard to tell whether you've acquired a new customer only as a result of your presence at a trade show. They may already have seen your ads or other marketing materials, for instance. And sometimes the new business generated by trade show leads comes in long after the show is over. That's why some people prefer to set a target ROO (Return On Objective) instead. With an ROO, your measure of success isn't restricted to a dollar amount: If you go to a show with the objective of generating 30 leads and you do that, then your ROO has been achieved.

Trade Show Goals

Use this worksheet to list potential trade show goals for your business.

What is your primary trade show goal?

What is your secondary trade show goal?

What are your other trade show goals?

QUICK**TIP**

Word of Mouth

Don't make your trade show decisions in a vacuum. Talk to people in your industry—your customers, your competitors, other major players—about their show experiences. Odds are *someone* in your address book has already been to the shows and conferences you're considering, so ask around for tips and opinions.

4. Research potential shows

According to the Center for Exhibition Industry Research (CEIR), more than 14,000 trade shows and other exhibit opportunities take place each year in the United States, ranging from small association conferences to huge expos. So how do you find the right ones for you? Research.

Resources for finding out about potential shows include:

- **Online show databases.** Many trade show industry magazines, organizations, and associations boast searchable lists of shows and conferences. Look for directory links on sites like TradeshowWeek.com and TSNN.com (Trade Show News Network) to find lists of exhibit opportunities in your industry.
- **Internet search engines.** You may have just as much (or more) luck finding relevant shows and conferences by using a broad Internet search engine such as Google or Yahoo. Search for relevant industry keywords combined with terms like "trade show" or "conference." Of course, your results will be only as good as your search terms, so you may need to proceed by trial and error.
- **Industry associations.** Check your industry associations' websites for announcements about upcoming conferences and other events. The people who attend these shows are more likely to be in your target market than those who go to more broadly based shows.
- **Your customers.** Ask your current customers or clients which shows and conferences they attend. If a lot of them are going to the same ones, other people like them are likely attending, too. This means you'll have access to a great pool of potential customers.

- **Your competitors.** Find out what shows and conferences your competitors attend. You'll enhance your business image if you're seen at the same events. And if they're doing well at a particular show, you'll probably find good opportunities there, too. Your competitors may list the events they attend on their websites. If not, call and ask. The worst that can happen is that they won't tell you.
- **Consultants.** You can hire trade show consultants to analyze your options and suggest shows based on your goals and target market. Consultants come with a high price tag, though, so this isn't a realistic choice for small businesses getting started in the world of trade shows.

Potential Shows

Use this worksheet to list trade shows you've discovered that have good potential for your business.

___

___

___

___

___

___

___

___

___

___

___

Show Evaluation

Once you've narrowed down your list of potential shows, go back and gather more detailed data about each one. Most shows and conferences have their own websites, which usually include statistics and general information from past years. By drilling down to this next layer of data, you'll be able to compare and contrast shows at a glance. Then you can evaluate each potential choice.

Show Evaluation

Use this worksheet to gather specific data about your top show choices so you can evaluate each one.

Show Name:

Date:

Location:

Anticipated Attendance:

Number of Exhibitors:

Who Exhibits:

Cost to Exhibit:

Registration Deadline:

Show Name:

Date:

Location:

Anticipated Attendance:

Number of Exhibitors:

Who Exhibits:

Cost to Exhibit:

Show Name:

Date:

Location:

Anticipated Attendance:

Number of Exhibitors:

Who Exhibits:

Cost to Exhibit:

Registration Deadline:

Top Show Choices

Rank your top show choices by name, from strongest candidate to weakest. Give the reason for each ranking.

Rank	Show Name	Reason for Ranking

5. Your target customer

It's important to know what type of people you're trying to reach. This helps you decide what to take to the show, how to design your booth and marketing materials, and how to pitch your product or service. Every time you make a show-related decision, ask yourself, "How will this help me reach my target customer?"

Define your target audience by profiling your target customer. If your customer is an individual, consider:

- **Age.** How old is your target customer? (You can specify a range here.)
- **Income.** What is your target customer's income level?
- **Gender.** Are your target customers mostly men or women, or do you have approximately equal numbers of both?
- **Profession/job title.** Do your target customers have particular job titles or functions?
- **Purchasing power.** Do your target customers make the decision to purchase themselves or must they consult with others?
- **Education.** What level of education do your target customers have?
- **Family.** Are your target customers single? Married? Do they have children? If so, how many?
- **Beliefs.** What do your target customers believe about your product or service? About themselves?
- **Motivations.** Why will your target customers select your product or service over another?
- **Affiliations.** What groups, associations, or organizations do your target customers belong to?
- **Hobbies.** What hobbies do your target customers have?
- **Location.** Where do your target customers live or work?

If your customer is another company, consider:

- **Industry.** To what industries do your target customers belong? In what industries do they do business?
- **Company size.** How many employees, branches, or outlets do your target customers have?
- **Location.** Are your target customers local, national, international?
- **Revenue.** What annual revenue do your target customers have?
- **Budget.** How much will your target customers be willing to spend on your product or service?

- **Products/services.** Which products or services do your target customers sell?
- **Business style.** Do your target customers do business in a formal or an informal style?
- **Affiliations.** What groups, associations, or organizations do your target customers belong to?
- **Motivations.** Why will your target customers select your product or service over another?

Target Customer Profile

Use this worksheet to profile your target customers. Then rank the customer characteristics that are most important to you. The more top-rated characteristics show attendees have, the more likely they'll be target customers for your business.

Rank	Individual customers	Rank	Company customers
	Age:		Industry:
	Income:		Company size:
	Gender:		Location:
	Profession/job title:		Revenue:
	Purchasing power:		Budget:
	Education:		Products/services:
	Family:		Business style:
	Beliefs:		Affiliations:
	Motivations:		Motivations:
	Affiliations:		
	Hobbies:		
	Location:		

6. Identify potential target customers

Once you've profiled your ideal customer, it's time to put together a list of potential target customers who match that profile as closely as possible. It's important to do this before heading off to the trade show because you'll want to contact potential targets by phone, mail, or email as part of your pre-show promotion plan (see Step 3 for more). This will increase your odds of drawing qualified leads to your exhibit.

Some of the people or companies on your list may already be attending the show(s) you have in mind, but others may decide to sign up only after they hear of the event from you.

To develop your list of potential target customers to contact, consider the following sources:

- **Your own list of contacts.** Many businesses have a list of prospective customers or clients that they'd like to convert into actual customers or clients. These people should be at the top of your pre-show contact list. You already know you want to talk to them, so why not try to set an appointment during the show?
- **Show management.** Show management is the only reliable source of a list of verified show attendees. Because the list is one of their biggest assets, most show managers charge a fee (generally at least a few hundred dollars). Some, however, may give you past years' or pre-show attendee lists free of charge if you've already signed up as an exhibitor. Others may share attendees' general demographic information. If you decide to buy a list from show management, work with them to whittle it down to the attendees you're most interested in meeting. (To do this, use the information you established in your target profile.)
- **Trade (or industry) associations.** Industry associations are excellent sources of potential targets who are likely to fit your profile. If you're already a member and you have a directory listing your fellow members, you have an instant mailing list. If not, you'll likely have to pay for a list of contacts, just as you would for a list of show attendees.

- **Word of mouth.** Although the list of names generated by word of mouth isn't likely to be very long, it could make up for its brevity with its quality. If your industry contacts pass along potential targets' names, chances are they're doing so because they know the targets are likely to meet your customer criteria.
- **Trade press.** If you read your industry's trade magazines and newspapers, you'll likely keep coming across the same boldfaced names, time after time. Add these people to your list of potential targets. Getting the opportunity to meet one or two key players can sometimes justify your entire show investment.
- **Show speakers and sponsors.** The speakers and sponsors listed in the show guide will likely have attended the event before. They might be willing to give you some insight into the types of people who attend, and they might even offer you specific names. Pick up the phone or send an email asking speakers and sponsors for assistance. A little networking may go a long way.
- **Non-competitive exhibitors.** Ask show management for a list of previous exhibitors and contact a few who aren't direct competitors. They should be able to tell you who has attended shows in past years.

QUICK**TIP**

Start Small

If you're just starting out as an exhibitor, it's probably better to get a couple of shows under your belt before shelling out hundreds of dollars for a mailing list. Once you've spent a few days on a show floor talking to attendees, you'll have a much clearer idea of who you're really looking for. This will help you decide what kind of mailing list you want to buy.

Potential Target Customers

Use this worksheet to create a list of potential target customers to meet at the trade show.

Source	Name and Contact Information
My Own Contacts	
Show List	
Trade Associations	

Source	**Name and Contact Information**
Mailing Lists	
Word of Mouth	
Press	
Other	

"Most Wanted" List

After you've collected your list of potential targets, use this worksheet to create a shorter list of your top 10 to 20 "wish list" contacts. These are the people you *most* want to talk to at the trade show—because working with them will guarantee you lots of business or because they can introduce you to important people in your industry or for another reason. When it's time to do your pre-show promotion, you'll devote the most attention and energy to these people.

Target Name	**Company**	**Contact Information**	**Why They're Important**

STEP 1: Choose the Right Show

STEP 2: Book the Show

STEP 3: Create Promotion and Marketing Materials

STEP 4: Merchandise at Your Booth

STEP 5: Turn Browsers into Buyers

STEP 6: Think Outside the Booth

STEP 7: Follow-Up

STEP 8: Evaluate the Show

STEP 9: The Booth

STEP 10: Show Shipments

Accomplishments

In this step you'll:

- ☐ 1. Learn how to reserve exhibit space at a trade show
- ☐ 2. Learn how to estimate your show budget
- ☐ 3. Learn how to choose a location on the exhibit floor
- ☐ 4. Find out which show services you need—and which you don't
- ☐ 5. Learn how to plan for trade show travel and accommodations

Time-Saving Tools

You'll complete this step more quickly if you have the following handy:

- ☐ The "Top Show Choices" worksheet you completed in Step 1

Step 2:
Book the Show

Once you've selected a show (or multiple shows) at which you want to exhibit, you must reserve your exhibit space. Do this as soon as you've made the decision to attend a particular show. Many shows offer early-registration discounts, and space can fill up fast.

Registering for exhibit space is only the first of many logistical tasks you'll be completing as a trade show exhibitor. You also need to:

- Estimate your show budget
- Select your exhibit location
- Reserve the services you'll need in your booth
- Make travel and accomodation arrangements

There's a reason larger companies hire full-time trade show managers: staying on top of the details involved in attending a show is a lot of work. Since you are your company's trade show manager, it's important to stay organized and meet deadlines. This will ensure that you make the most of your trade show investment.

QUICK**TIP**

Stay Organized

You'll collect a lot of materials related to your trade show, so get organized:

- **Put everything in one place. A spiral-bound notebook works well. Use dividers to create sections for exhibit documentation, show services, and travel arrangements.**
- **File all new papers immediately. Don't throw away any show-related paperwork until after the show is over.**
- **Create a "master document." On a single sheet of paper, create a list of essential show information: dates, location, travel details, scheduled events, and meetings. Keep it in the front of your binder, give a copy to every employee attending the show, and update it as necessary.**

QUICK**TIP**

Register Online

Many shows allow—and often encourage—exhibitors to register online. Sometimes online registration is available weeks or months before paperwork is sent out. This lets you get a jump on planning. If you do reserve your exhibit space online, print out and save hard copies of every form you submit. Call to confirm that your reservation has been received and take your forms to the show as proof of the services and features you ordered.

1. Make the reservations

Once you decide to exhibit at a particular show or conference, you need to reserve your spot on the show floor. The reservation process itself is actually fairly straightforward once you know:

- **Who to contact.** Associations usually have an exhibitor relations department or representative, while large conventions and expos have a show management team. The fastest way to find the contact name is to go to the website of the show or conference and navigate to the exhibitors' section.
- **What they send you.** When you reach the show contact, ask them to send you the show's vital statistics—dates, deadlines, pricing, number of attendees—as well as the required sign-up paperwork. You'll receive a packet or binder with everything you need to participate in the show: registration forms, payment information, sponsorship opportunities, booth service options, shipping details, and so on. More shows are sending this kind of information via email, but many still send out packets and binders.

- **How to register.** The most important form you'll receive is your exhibitor registration form. (There's no single, standardized term for this document, so it may be called something else in the materials you receive.) Fill out this form and return it with payment of your registration fee. Faxing the form has two advantages. It allows you to follow up later that day to make sure the form was received, and it lets you keep the original copy. File it with your show paperwork.

- **When to register.** Reserve your exhibit space as soon as you're certain you're going to exhibit at the show. Many shows and conferences offer early-registration discounts (up to 10%). Early registrants may also be able to take advantage of special "turnkey" packages that include exhibit space plus a bundled set of services/features for one price. Many shows also include exhibitors' names and/or logos on their website before the show. The sooner you sign up, the sooner your information will be online for potential attendees to see.

QUICK**TIP**

Better Late Than Never

Reserving your space early has many advantages. But if you don't find out about the perfect show until just a few weeks before it starts, don't let a tight deadline keep you from exhibiting. For some shows, "early" registration periods don't end until a month or so before the show begins. Even if you can't get an early-registration discount, it's worth paying the full price to be at a show that's good for your business.

2. Estimate your show budget

Attending a trade show isn't cheap. The money you spend on your exhibit space, your booth (see Step 9), your pre- and post-show promotional campaign (see Step 3), travel, and other costs adds up quickly. What's more, average trade show expenses increase 10% every year, thanks to higher rental fees and other associated costs.

According to *Tradeshow Week* magazine, the average cost per square foot of trade show exhibit space in 2006 was just over $23. Since exhibit space rental accounts for approximately 30% of the average show cost, you can do a rough budget estimate by multiplying the cost of your exhibit space by three. For a more detailed estimate, use the worksheet on pages 32-33.

Aside from exhibit space rental, where does your trade show dollar go? The chart below will give you an idea.

TYPE OF EXPENSE	APPROXIMATE PERCENTAGE OF TRADE SHOW BUDGET
Exhibit space	25%-35%
Booth construction	12%-18%
Show services (such as carpet rental and electricity)	12%-20%
Shipping/transportation	10%
Promotion	6%-10%
Travel/accommodation	18%-21%

Get the Most for Your Money

Exhibiting at a trade show is expensive. But as the old saying goes, sometimes you have to spend money to make money. Meeting even one highly qualified new prospect can sometimes justify your entire trade show investment.

To maximize your budget:

- **Plan ahead.** Most shows and conferences offer discounts on exhibit space rental and show services if you reserve early. Some also offer flat-rate packages to early registrants, bundling a set list of services with exhibit space rental.
- **Negotiate.** If exhibitors aren't banging down their doors to sign up, show management may be willing to deal. You could offer to sign up as an exhibitor for a certain number of years at a reduced rate. You might also see if you can get an all-inclusive price for your space and services.
- **Think small and lightweight.** Keep the amount of exhibit space you rent to a minimum (few companies need more than the standard 10' x 10' space). And when buying a booth, opt for a lightweight system. The lighter your booth, the cheaper it will be to ship.
- **Eliminate the booth.** If you're going to be exhibiting at more than three shows per year, buying a booth is a smart investment. If not, consider renting (a basic rental is usually 25%–30% of the cost of a new booth), buying used (20%–50% of the cost of new), or getting an inexpensive vinyl backdrop instead (these can cost as little as $100).
- **Take your own equipment.** Renting extension cords and power strips from show management is expensive. As long as you won't be breaking any show rules, take your own. If a handheld vacuum fits in your luggage, toss that in, too, or buy a carpet sweeper from a local store when you arrive. Then you can skip the booth cleaning service.
- **Handle set-up yourself.** While most shows (especially larger ones) technically require exhibitors to use contracted labor to set up exhibits, an unwritten industry rule allows small exhibitors to set up their own booths as long as it doesn't take more than 30 minutes. Practice ahead of time so you can set up quickly.

Trade Show Budget

Use this worksheet to estimate your trade show budget. After you've exhibited, fill in the "actual cost" column so you'll have an even more accurate guide for next time.

ITEM	EST. COST	ACTUAL COST
EXHIBIT COSTS		
Exhibit space	$	$
Booth rental (if applicable)	$	$
Other exhibit fees (registration, badges)	$	$
SUBTOTAL	$	$
SHOW SERVICES		
Electricity	$	$
Carpet/flooring	$	$
Cleaning	$	$
Furniture rental	$	$
Internet access	$	$
Equipment rental (computer, TV, trash can, telephone, extension cords)	$	$
Plants	$	$
Lighting	$	$
Other show services	$	$
SUBTOTAL	$	$
BOOTH PURCHASE		
Design costs	$	$
Construction costs	$	$
Graphics	$	$
Lighting	$	$
Cost of used booth (if applicable)	$	$
SUBTOTAL	$	$

ITEM	**EST. COST**	**ACTUAL COST**
SHIPPING/TRANSPORTATION		
Booth shipping costs (outbound)	$	$
Other materials shipping costs (outbound)	$	$
Booth shipping costs (inbound)	$	$
Other materials shipping costs (inbound)	$	$
Drayage/at-show transportation costs	$	$
Storage	$	$
Insurance	$	$
SUBTOTAL	$	$
PROMOTION/LEAD GATHERING		
Pre-show contact (phone calls, mailings)	$	$
Mailing list rental	$	$
Marketing material/literature (such as catalogs, brochures)	$	$
Giveaways	$	$
Lead cards or trade show notebooks	$	$
Product demonstration preparation/materials	$	$
Show sponsorship (includes program ads)	$	$
Press releases	$	$
Follow-up contact (phone calls, mailings)	$	$
SUBTOTAL	$	$
TRAVEL/ACCOMMODATION		
Airfare	$	$
Hotel	$	$
Rental car/taxis	$	$
Food and entertainment	$	$
SUBTOTAL	$	$
PERSONNEL		
Booth staff salary	$	$
Staff training	$	$
Apparel	$	$
SUBTOTAL	$	$
TOTAL	$	$

QUICK**TIP**

Plan Ahead

A fancy booth with eye-catching graphics and hanging signs has a lot of appeal. But exhibitors have been known to acquire such items only to discover they won't fit in the space provided at the convention center! Before you make the same mistake, inquire about the dimensions of the exhibition hall and make sure your exhibit will fit in the allotted space.

3. Choose your booth location

Many show organizers ask exhibitors to choose their booth locations when they register. Depending on how show management has divided up the space, you may be limited to certain areas based on the size of your booth and/or your segment of the industry. And in some cases, you won't have much choice in the matter at all, especially if you're a small or first-time exhibitor.

If you are in a position to select your booth location, these tips will help you choose the best space available.

Do:

- **Try for a corner.** Because spaces where two aisles meet have twice the aisle real estate, they get more traffic than regular, in-line spots. If you end up in a corner space, take any side rails down and make sure your tables are draped on all sides.
- **Aim for the center.** The center of the exhibit floor is where most of the action takes place. So if your goal is to generate a lot of traffic, get as close to the center as possible.
- **Lean to the right.** According to psychologists, people naturally tend to angle to the right when they enter a big space like an exhibition hall. So if your booth is on the right side of the floor, you may get more foot traffic.
- **Piggyback.** If you want to draw a crowd, angle for a space near a large exhibitor. Being close to a big booth that's teeming with activity brings in visitors.

Don't:

- **Go front and center.** People peel off to the left and right when they enter an exhibition hall. They might be halfway down the first aisle before they even look around to see where they are. So if you're directly opposite the main entrance, you could get passed by.
- **End up on the fringes.** If you're far away from the main action, some attendees will never make it to your booth.
- **Compete with necessities for attention.** If you're beside the food concessions and/or restrooms, people will zoom past you to get to them. Big crowds of non-qualified people may also form near your booth, crowding out real leads.
- **Get stranded.** Being anywhere except in the main exhibition hall isn't a good idea. Try to avoid getting stuck in a space that's off the beaten path or in a thoroughfare for attendees on their way to the main event. Also watch out for obstacles like columns and stairs.

In the end, the best location for your booth depends on your objective. If you have many appointments set, opt for a quieter area. If you want to meet the highest number of people, aim for a high-traffic zone. But by inviting key leads, contacts, and target customers to your booth before the show even starts, you can succeed wherever you are placed. As long as your pre-show promotion plan is thorough and well executed (see Step 3), your exact location may not matter too much.

QUICK**TIP**

Do Some Detective Work

Do a little research to find out what other exhibitors will be at the show—and, more importantly, *where* they'll be. Ask show management for that information, then try to claim a spot near exhibitors whose products or services complement your own. This will help draw potential customers to your booth.

Exhibit Space Sizes and Types

The smallest exhibit space at most shows is a 10' x 10' square along one of the aisles. Known as an "in-line" booth because of its location, the 10' x10' booth is typical for businesses without large trade show budgets.

In-line spaces along the outer walls of the show floor are known as "perimeter booths," and spots at the end of the aisle are called "corner booths" because they're open on two sides. Larger, more expensive in-line options (10' x 15', 10' x 20', and even 10' x 30') with the extra square footage giving you more frontage on the aisle, rather than more depth, are usually available as well. Exhibitors renting more than 300 square feet can take advantage of more flexible space options:

- **Peninsula booths** stretch across the entire end of an aisle, which means they're open to traffic on three sides.
- **Island booths** are usually reserved for the largest exhibitors. These booths stand alone in a large open space, often in the center of the show floor. Island exhibitors are usually allowed to hang larger, more noticeable graphics and signs above their booths, which get them a lot of attendee attention.

If your products take up a lot of physical space and/or you're looking to make a big splash in your industry, you can consider paying more for a bigger space or a more desirable location on the floor. But if you're just starting out and your main goal is to meet qualified leads, a 10' x 10' in-line is all you need.

4. Show services

Never assume *anything* when it comes to show services. Nothing automatically comes along with your exhibit space. The only things that are definitely free of charge are the overhead lights on the ceiling of the exhibition hall and the carpet under your feet (that is, if it's a carpeted room to begin with). If the room isn't carpeted, you'll be paying for the carpet, too! Everything else needs to be ordered from show management or supplied by you.

Although exhibitors go through the exhibition organizers to choose the services they do and do not want, in many cases, these are offered by vendors who have contracts with the show. "Turnkey" packages are often available to exhibitors who register early. These packages bundle a particular set of services together with exhibit space. They might include a 10' x 10' space, carpeting, a draped table, a listing on the show's website and in the show program, and a few badges for the people working your booth.

The services you choose depend on show management, as well as on your exhibit and show objectives. Note that some services may be mandatory. *Always* obey the rules and regulations in your show manual.

QUICK**TIP**

Read the Signs

Show management won't provide anything in your exhibit space that identifies your company, except, perhaps, a small sign bearing your company's name and booth number. So be sure to take your own signage to the show.

SERVICE	WHAT IS IT?	DO YOU NEED IT?	WHY OR WHY NOT?
Exhibit Installation & Dismantling (I&D)	Technically, exhibitors are required to use show management's contracted labor vendor to set up and take down their booths.	Maybe	Most shows follow the unwritten "30-Minute Rule," which gives small exhibitors 30 minutes to set up their own booths. So if you have a small booth, you may be able to do this. But if you have a large, complicated exhibit, it's hard to avoid I&D.
Back wall and side draping	In order to separate you from the exhibits next door to and behind you, most shows hang fabric panels at the back and sides of the exhibit space. Traditionally, back wall and side draping is provided for all exhibitors as part of their space, but check to be sure.	Yes	Without draping, your exhibit space won't have any borders, which not only looks bad but also causes confusion. Sometimes you can choose the color of the drape.
Carpet/ flooring	Most convention centers have bare, concrete floors. If you want something else in your booth, you'll have to pay for it. Carpet is the most popular trade show flooring option, but other choices (foam, linoleum, hardwood) may be available.	Yes	Bare, concrete floors are ugly and uncomfortable. Unless you buy and ship your own custom flooring, carpet is a must-have. Pick a color that goes with your display. You can save money by choosing the most inexpensive flooring option and skipping the extra padding.

SERVICE	WHAT IS IT?	DO YOU NEED IT?	WHY OR WHY NOT?
Furniture	Furniture options are varied, but the basics include a draped/skirted table and at least one chair. Larger exhibitors sometimes also rent sofas and conference tables.	Yes	It's almost always cheaper to rent furniture than to ship it. If you don't get a table with your exhibit space and your booth doesn't include a means of displaying products, you need a draped table. It's good for display, and you can also store things under the drape. Chairs are also a good idea. You'll need to sit down to rest at times, and you may need them for meetings.
Display aids	Need a rack to display your promotional materials? An extra stand for your product sample? Show management can rent you anything you need to organize your booth.	No	If you have a specific need for large racks, shelves, or stands, consider purchasing them. Otherwise, use the top of your table to display materials and product samples. To hold them, buy easels at an art supply store.
Electricity	To power your booth lights, your computer, and any other electric equipment, you need to order electricity. For your money, you'll get a single outlet wired to your exhibit location.	Yes	Lighting is an essential part of creating an appealing booth, and many exhibitors rely on computer or other electrically powered demonstrations. Save money by taking your own extension cords and power strips.

SERVICE	WHAT IS IT?	DO YOU NEED IT?	WHY OR WHY NOT?
Lighting	Many shows rent lights to exhibitors who need more or didn't bring any with them.	No	Take your own. Most booths come with some sort of lighting system. You can also improvise with inexpensive clip lights.
Plumbing	Exhibits that incorporate sinks or other water-based appliances in their displays need to secure plumbing services.	No	Unless running water is an essential part of your product demonstration, this is an unnecessary expense.
Wastebasket	People need a place to dump their empty coffee cups, used napkins, and other trash.	No	Take or buy your own. You can either ship it home or leave it behind.
Cleaning	Every night, show custodians will vacuum your exhibit space, empty your wastebasket, and remove other trash.	Probably	Some exhibitors take a handheld vacuum cleaner to the show and take care of their own cleaning. If you don't order cleaning, you'll be responsible for emptying your own wastebaskets, too.
Telephone line (and telephone)	Exhibitors can have an active phone line run to their space. Renting a phone to go with it is an additional expense.	No	Most calls can wait until you're out of the booth. If you think you'll need to make calls while you're on the show floor, use your cell phone instead.

SERVICE	WHAT IS IT?	DO YOU NEED IT?	WHY OR WHY NOT?
Internet connection	Even if the hotel has wireless Internet in the rooms, the connection may not work on the show floor. If you want to go online in your booth, you'll have to pay for it.	No	If you don't absolutely need this service for your demos, check your email at an Internet café or in your room.
Computer rental	Exhibitors can rent computers to use for demonstrations and/or to connect to the Internet.	No	Unless there's a strong security risk, take your own computer.
Audiovisual rental	You can rent large TVs, VCRs, DVD players, projectors, and any other equipment required for in-booth demonstrations.	Probably not	If you need a large TV or a DVD player to run your demo, renting makes sense. If you find yourself renting AV equipment frequently, it might be cheaper in the long run to buy and ship your own.
Photography	Most large shows have contracts with professional photographers who take high-quality photos of exhibitors' booths.	Probably not	Unless you need professional-quality photos for your website or promotional materials, you can take them yourself.
Host/hostess	You can hire models to stand outside your booth (or roam the show floor) to encourage attendees to stop by your exhibit.	No	For small exhibitors, this is an unnecessary expense.

SERVICE	WHAT IS IT?	DO YOU NEED IT?	WHY OR WHY NOT?
Lead retrieval system	Ranging from simple business card scanners to complicated computer kiosks, lead retrieval systems offer high-tech ways for you to capture data about qualified leads.	Probably not	If you don't think paper lead forms and old-fashioned notetaking will work for you, consider renting a business card scanner.
Security cages	These are mesh containers with locks that give you a place to secure valuables in your booth.	Maybe	If you need to keep valuables safe while you're away from your booth, a locked security cage may be a good option.
Flowers/ plants	You can rent plants and order fresh flowers for your booth.	No	Plants and flowers are pretty, but not necessities.
Catering	Exhibitors can have food and beverages delivered to their booths.	No	No food should be in your booth apart from product samples (if your product is edible) and/or snacks for booth staffers.

When you're just starting out as an exhibitor, stick to basic services like carpeting, electricity, table and chair rental, and possibly booth cleaning. Once you become more familiar with your needs and understand the workings of the trade show world, you can add more.

Show Services

Use this worksheet to prioritize the services you need at your booth.

Show Service	Must-Have	Optional	Don't Need
Exhibit Installation & Dismantling (I&D)			
Back wall and side draping			
Carpet/flooring			
Furniture			
Display aids			
Electricity			
Lighting			
Plumbing			
Wastebasket			
Cleaning			
Telephone line (and telephone)			
Internet connection			
Computer rental			
Audio/visual rental			
Photography			
Host/hostess			
Lead retrieval system			
Security cages			
Flowers/plants			
Catering			

QUICK**TIP**

Travel Smart

Check for discounts on hotel rooms, rental cars, and even plane tickets offered by show organizers. For large events, they often arrange for group rates for exhibitors and attendees.

5. Arrange travel and accommodation

Unless you're fortunate enough to find the ideal exhibit opportunity nearby, going to a show or convention means traveling. So book early. Start looking at plane tickets and hotel rooms as soon as you've reserved your exhibit space. Travel and accommodation will be more expensive as the time of the show approaches.

If you can, plan to arrive the day before the show opens and leave the day after it closes. You'll be much more relaxed, you'll have more time to meet with clients and other contacts, and delays will be less likely to affect your show experience. The last thing you want is to encounter a delay in your outbound flight that prevents you from arriving in time to set up your booth.

You'll need to stay overnight for most exhibitions. Your best option is usually the hotel where the show is taking place. If the event is being held in a convention center, stay at the hotel the show organizers have designated for official accommodation. The convenience of being in the same location as the exhibition hall far outweighs the savings of less expensive rooms farther from the venue. And if you stay at an off-site location, you'll spend plenty of money just getting yourself to and from the show location.

A few more useful accommodation tips:

- **Take advantage of mass transit.** If you can't (or decide not to) book a room at the convention hotel, look for one that has good access to mass transit. That way you won't have to rent a car or take cabs to get around. Some large shows have their own shuttle routes. If that's the case, try to stay near the shuttle stops.

QUICK**TIP**

Pack Smart

When you're traveling to and from the show, carry essentials with you. On your way to the show, that includes everything you'd need to function if none of your shipped goods showed up: business cards, electronic and hard copies of your promotional materials, and your show paperwork. On the way home, don't let anything you can't reproduce out of your sight, particularly data on your newly acquired sales leads. After all, they're the reason you went to the show in the first place!

- **Get your own room.** Many small companies try to cut show-related expenses by doubling up staff in hotel rooms. If that's all you can afford *and* your relationship with your co-worker(s) is strong enough to stand close quarters, it's an option. But if your budget can accommodate additional rooms, book them. Trade show days are long, and after spending hours on your feet talking to strangers, you will not likely be in the mood to bunk down in the same room as a co-worker.
- **Go to bed early.** Go to bed as early as you can. Trade shows are tiring, and you'll need to recharge.

Eat Smart

Meals are an important part of any trade show experience. Some are included as part of the exhibition package. Don't miss out on them. They provide fantastic opportunities for networking. And there are other ways to make the most of mealtimes:

- **Use meals for one-on-one meetings with clients or prospects.** People are usually more relaxed outside the exhibition hall. (See Step 6 for more tips on using mealtimes to your advantage.)
- **Eat a good breakfast.** If you're the only person staffing your exhibit, finding time to eat lunch can be difficult. Foot traffic also tends to increase around mealtimes, when attendees are not in seminar sessions.
- **Snack smart.** Stock your booth with bottled water and easy-to-eat snacks like granola bars. Avoid anything sticky or smelly (like oranges).

NOTES:

STEP 3: Create Promotion and Marketing Materials

Accomplishments

In this step you'll:

☐ 1. Learn who to contact before the show, how to contact them, when to contact them, and what to tell them

☐ 2. Learn which marketing materials to create and take to the show

Time-Saving Tools

You'll complete this step more quickly if you have the following handy:

☐ The "Target Profile" worksheet you completed in Step 1

☐ The "Potential Target Customers" worksheet you completed in Step 1

☐ The "Most Wanted List" worksheet you completed in Step 1

Step 3: Create Promotion and Marketing Materials

You wouldn't expect a new retail store to just wait for customers to walk through its doors. That's what "coming soon" and "grand opening" ads and fliers are for. For the same reason, it's important for trade show exhibitors to get the word out to attendees ahead of time. About 75 percent of show attendees plan their booth visits before the show starts, and you want to be part of their plans. So before the show date, invite plenty of people to visit your booth. The more you invite ahead of time, the greater the chances you'll have visits from strong potential customers during the event.

A good strategic pre-show promotion plan can have a great influence on the success of your trade show experience. Send out a simple email or postcard telling potential leads that you'll be at the show, and ask them to stop by your booth. Ads, press releases, and newsletters are other useful pre-show promotional vehicles. And don't forget the power of offering desirable giveaways.

Your promotional opportunities won't end once you're at the show. Use show sponsorships and printed marketing materials to get your message out and to make it stick.

QUICK**TIP**

Always Include Contact Information

Make sure your contact information appears on all pre-show promotional material you send out and on every piece you take to the show. Include:

- Your name
- Your company's name
- Your company website URL
- Your email address
- Your telephone number

QUICK**TIP**

Get Them to Your Booth

The minute attendees register and pick up their badges, show management has no more obligation to get people to the show. At that point, it's up to you to attract qualified leads to your booth. That's why it's so important to put your company's name on their radar before they arrive.

1. Pre-show promotion

Even if you have the fanciest booth in the exhibition hall, you won't draw in potential leads simply by signing up for a space and setting up a booth. Yes, you'll meet passersby, but they may not fit the target profile you set up in Step 1. You'll have a much better chance of success if you recruit visitors ahead of time. To set up an effective pre-show promotion plan, you'll need to know:

- Who to contact
- How to contact them
- When to contact them
- What to tell them

Who to Contact

In addition to your existing customers and contacts, your pre-show promotion plan should include anyone who might be attending the show and anyone who fits your target profile. Potential leads come from a variety of sources, including (but not limited to):

- Show management (the only reliable source for confirmed attendees)
- Industry associations
- Industry publications
- Your own contact database
- Word of mouth
- Other exhibitors

QUICK**TIP**

How to Boost Attendance

Include your current customers in your pre-show promotion plan. Hearing about the show from you may encourage them to attend if they aren't already signed up. Your pre-show contact serves as a reminder not only of your existing relationship and of any new products or services you have to offer, but also of the show itself.

Renting or buying a mailing list from show management or an association usually isn't cheap. However, some shows will give you a list of past attendees free of charge, and others will pass on current attendees' information once you've confirmed your status as an exhibitor. Ask show management what information they can offer you.

If you do rent or buy any large contact lists, go through them carefully to choose the attendees most likely to fit your target profile. Don't waste time or money contacting people who aren't potential leads. (See pages 20-21 for more on who to contact.)

How to Contact Them

Once you've compiled your list of potential targets, you're ready to contact them. The easiest and cheapest way to do this is to send an email (see page 56 for a sample message or letter). Email is easy to personalize, costs much less than sending a letter, and can be dressed up to include pictures and logos.

Other ways to contact people before the show:

- Postcards
- Letters
- Company newsletters
- Updates posted on your company website (announcing your presence at the show, your booth number, and any special products, features, or promotions you'll be offering)
- Directory listing on the show's website
- Ads/listings in show newsletters/email updates

QUICK**TIP**

Use Freebies!

Be sure to take advantage of any promotional opportunities that don't put a dent in your bottom line. Many shows and conferences include materials like online directory listings in their exhibitor registration packages, so read your agreement thoroughly to see what you're getting. Then make sure you get it.

Other promotional tricks that won't cost you a dime: adding show-related news and information to your own company website and including it in any mailings you'd be sending anyway (including newsletters and fliers announcing specials and sales).

- Ads in trade publications (journals, magazines, newspapers)
- Press releases
- Billboards on main traffic routes to the event location

All of these options are fairly cheap—apart from the last one, which is splashy, but not realistic for most companies.

When to Contact Them

Large companies with full-time trade show managers start contacting big customers and potential clients up to 90 days before an upcoming event. But that's not really necessary for smaller exhibitors. Many attendees wait until the last minute to register. Unless your message or mailer is extraordinarily memorable, it's going to be forgotten if you send it that far in advance.

A more realistic timeline for your pre-show promotion plan (for a full trade show timeline, see pages 168-169):

- **One month before the show:** Send your initial email/mailing.
- **Two weeks before the show:** Send your second email/mailing (this can be similar to the first one, with a "don't forget" angle).
- **One to two days before the show:** Send a last-minute reminder email to confirmed attendees/anyone who responded to your previous mailings.

What to Tell Them

Think of your initial pre-show mailing as both an announcement and an invitation. Give your leads two key messages: (1) you'll be at the show and (2) you want them to visit your booth.

Other important points to keep in mind when composing your pre-show mailings:

- **Be clear about your target audience.** If you've screened them carefully, most of the people on your contact list fit your target customer profile, but there are bound to be some on the borderline. You can weed them out ahead of time by mentioning your specific audience in the mailer. Use "Calling all food service buyers!" as a subject line, for example. Those who aren't buyers will know that your booth isn't for them, saving you the effort of trying to figure out whether they're qualified leads at the show itself.

Make Appointments Ahead of Time

To be sure you see your existing customers and other contacts during a show, make appointments with them ahead of time. Start the scheduling process before your other pre-show promotional activities. That way, people will still have lots of room in their calendars. Ideally, this is as soon as you know they'll be attending the show. The appointments you set can be as simple as agreeing on a specific day and time for a visit to your booth. But for your best clients or any key leads you've identified, try to plan for a more relaxed meeting outside the booth: coffee, dinner, or another outing. And be sure to exchange full contact information when you agree on a meeting time. Schedules often change at the last minute, so you may need to get in touch again before the event.

QUICK**TIP**

Tell Them Your Booth Number

If show management assigns you a specific exhibit space number ahead of time, include it in *all* of your pre-show promotion materials, from emails to ads in trade journals. The more times attendees see your company name next to that number before they get to the show, the more likely they are to remember it.

- **Give attendees a good reason to visit your booth.** Extol the benefits of your product or service (rather than its features), promote a new product, or offer special show pricing. Simply including your company's name and booth number in your mailings won't give them enough incentive to pay a visit.
- **Make it personal.** With computers making mail-merge programs fast and easy, your email will be more effective if you address each pre-show mailing you send directly to the recipient. (Postcards, however, are an exception.

Front of a pre-show promotion postcard.

Calling all business and entrepreneurship professors!

Looking for an addition to your class syllabus? The Planning Shop, publisher of the bestselling *Successful Business Plan: Secrets and Strategies*, will debut its latest indispensable guide, *Trade Show In A Day*, at the

2006 United States Small Business Expo

March 30 – April 1, 2006

For more information, visit:

www.planningshop.com

We look forward to seeing you at **Booth 150**!

They're more like ads and so are less personal than letters to begin with.) Make sure your sign-off is personal, too. Include your name and signature.

- **Mention any show sponsorships or special events you're involved in.** If you're paying for a sponsorship, get more mileage out of it by noting it in your pre-show mailers. The same goes for any speaking engagements or presentations you're participating in at the show. Invite your contacts to those events as well as to your booth.

QUICK**TIP**

Advertise on the Cheap

If you can't afford a sponsorship, consider placing an ad in the show program. The closer you get to the show, the cheaper this space will be, since show management will want to fill up all the available spots. If you buy an ad, make sure your company name/logo and booth number are prominent. That's the most important information to convey to attendees.

Back of a pre-show promotion postcard.

thePlanningshop™

Join us at the 2006 U.S. Small Business Expo

Where: The Montecito, Las Vegas, Nevada

When: March 30-April 1, 2006

For more information, visit: www.planningshop.com

Come visit us at **Booth 150** and sign up for your FREE desk copy of *Trade Show In A Day*.

Plus, don't miss our very own Rhonda Abrams, who will be speaking at the Keynote Session on Thursday, March 30.

We look forward to seeing you at **Booth 150**!

TO:

QUICK**TIP**

Be Smart About Your Subject Line

With so much spam clogging email in-boxes, it's important to make sure the subject lines of your pre-show emails aren't vague or suspicious. Include the show name as well as your company name.

thePlanningshop

2006 United States Small Business Expo:
An invitation from The Planning Shop

Dear NAME,

Greetings from The Planning Shop!

I'm writing to invite you to visit our booth at the upcoming U.S. Small Business Expo, where we'll debut our latest indispensable guide, *Trade Show In A Day*. Like our previous bestsellers, *Six Week Start-Up* and *What Business Should I Start?*, it's sure to be an invaluable addition to your class materials.

That's why we'd like to offer you a FREE desk copy of *Trade Show In A Day* at the Conference. Just stop by **Booth 150** to sign up.

Where: The Montecito, Las Vegas, Nevada
When: March 30–April 1, 2006
For more information, visit: www.planningshop.com

I'd also like to invite you to attend my talk at the Keynote Session on Thursday, March 30.

I look forward to seeing you at the Expo!

Best wishes,

Rhonda Abrams, CEO
The Planning Shop
www.PlanningShop.com

P.S. Don't forget to stop by **Booth 150** to sign up for your FREE desk copy of *Trade Show In A Day*!

Sample of a pre-show promotion email or letter.

Show Sponsorship

Once you register for a show or conference, show management may send you sponsorship forms. Sponsorships are opportunities for you to pay to put your logo on show-related advertising or promotional material.

Depending on the size of the show and what you sponsor, sponsorships cost from $250 to over $100,000. As a general rule, if you want your name on an item that every attendee receives (as opposed to something that's handed out to only a few), you will have to pay more.

Depending on how much you pay for a sponsorship, you will have access to a wide range of promotional opportunities, including (but certainly not limited to):

QUICK**TIP**

The Secret Language of Sponsorships

Many shows name different types of sponsorships after precious metals or stones: bronze, silver, gold, platinum, diamond, emerald, and so on. The more precious the stone or metal, the more expensive the sponsorship.

- An active link on the show's website (this is a must for *any* sponsorship level)
- Ads in newsletters that go out to everyone attending the show and/or everyone on the organizing body's mailing list
- Your company's name on any presentation that's displayed on screen at group events
- Your marketing materials pre-loaded into event tote bags
- Your company's name/logo on badge holders
- Your name on the event tote bag
- The opportunity to speak at an educational session or other show event
- The chance to host show parties, dinners, breakfasts, or coffee service, where your logo is prominently displayed on signs and/or cups and napkins and your staff can mingle with attendees

For smaller companies, sponsorships are generally worthwhile only at shows with a small, highly targeted group of attendees. Otherwise, anything you can afford to sponsor will be dwarfed by the mega-sponsorships of larger exhibitors. Sign up for sponsorships as early as possible so your company name and logo can be included in all the updates show management sends out before the event.

View a sponsorship as you would any other purchase. What kind of visibility will you have as a sponsor? Will you be recognized on the show's website? Will you be given a chance to speak or run a session?

One other thing to consider: Paying for a sponsorship may result in a better relationship with—and better service from—show management. And, as a sponsor, you may be allowed to take more staffers to the show.

Pre-Show Promotion Plan

Use this worksheet to brainstorm ideas for your pre-show promotion plan.

List potential sources of contact names for pre-show mailings:

List contacts you'd like to set appointments with before the show:

List key prospects who might be candidates for special giveaways. List ideas for giveaways and coupon offers:

List any free promotional opportunities you can take advantage of:

List any sponsorships you're considering:

Use a separate sheet of paper to draft the text of your pre-show postcard.

Use a separate sheet of paper to draft the text of your pre-show email.

2. Marketing materials

Some trade show veterans question the need to take *any* printed marketing materials to a show. They argue that many price sheets and catalogs are soon tossed and that you can mail or email materials after the show to attendees who request them.

It's true that many trade show handouts end up in the trash. And you certainly can send extra materials to those who ask for them. But attendees come to trade shows to gather information. The people you meet in your booth need *something* they can take home with them to remind them about you and what you talked about. If they don't take something, they'll forget you before they arrive at the next booth.

So rather than forgo materials altogether, be smart about what you take. If you keep your materials minimal and easy to carry, you'll meet attendees' need for information without burying them under a mountain of paper.

Putting Your Materials on CD?

Unless you're in a high-tech industry, think twice before putting your promotional materials on a CD or DVD. CDs and DVDs are expensive to produce, and they're often the first things to be tossed when attendees clean out their tote bags. Unless prospects are *very* interested in your products or services, they won't likely make the effort to load the disk into their computers. If you do opt for audiovisual materials, prepare a one-page informational handout, too.

QUICK**TIP**

Keep a Copy of Everything

Don't ever give away your last copy of any piece of marketing material! If you start to run low on easily reprintable items (single-page sales sheets, for example), make extras at a local copy shop. Even if you're down to your last catalog, don't let it go. Have someone back at the office send more overnight. If no one is available to do that for you, promise to send interested attendees their own copies as soon as the conference is over. And if you are shipping items ahead, *always* take an electronic and a hard copy of everything with you to the event in case your shipment goes astray.

These guidelines will help you decide what to take to the show:

TYPE OF MATERIAL	INFORMATION TO INCLUDE	HOW MANY TO TAKE	WHO GETS THEM	WHEN TO HAND THEM OUT
Single-sheet handout	Special offers, products, themes, or show discounts you're promoting. You can make up individual sheets for different products. These handouts don't have to be in color, but they should look good.	For a highly targeted show, take 50% of the total number of expected attendees (so if 100 people are attending, take 50). For a more general show, take 10%–20% of the expected number of attendees.	Anyone who wants one.	Whenever someone expresses interest in your company/products. Leave a pile on a table for people to pick up.
Catalog	Details on your entire product line. (These are usually four-color, glossy publications.)	For a highly targeted show, take 10%–30% of the total number of expected attendees. For a more general show, take 1%–10% of the expected number of attendees.	Key leads and hot prospects.	When you meet with an attendee who is a strong prospective customer. These can also be mailed after the show.
Price list	A list of current prices for your products/services. Using stand-alone price sheets saves you the expense of printing updated catalogs for every event.	See catalog, above.	See catalog, above.	With catalogs.

TYPE OF MATERIAL	INFORMATION TO INCLUDE	HOW MANY TO TAKE	WHO GETS THEM	WHEN TO HAND THEM OUT
Brochure	Promotional material about your company and your products. Include information about your mission, your history, and any honors you've received. Can be a standard tri-fold brochure or a two-sided glossy sheet.	A small number. None if you are taking catalogs.	See catalog, above.	With catalogs.
Business card	Your contact information, including name, title, company name, email address, phone number(s), fax number(s), website URL. Use a standard size, since people collect them in standard-size holders.	250–500, depending on the size of the show.	Leads or contacts you speak with personally.	At the end of your conversation with a lead or contact. You can leave some out for pickup at your booth, but in general, reserve cards for personal exchanges.

QUICK**TIP**

Don't Overpack

If you know 10,000 people will be at a show, you don't need to take 10,000 brochures. Not every attendee is going to come by your booth, and even those who do aren't going to take a copy of everything you have. See the chart on pages 60-61 for general quantity guidelines.

Other printed materials to take:

- Order forms and invoices (if you plan to take orders at your booth)
- Lead forms (see page 89)

About 6 months before the show, start planning which marketing materials you want to take (and how many). Print them about 2 to 3 months before the show so you can have them packed up and ready to ship a month ahead of time.

Printed Promotional Materials Checklist

Use this worksheet to keep track of the number and type of marketing materials you plan to take to the show.

Type of Material	Taking to the Show?	Number
Single-page handout		
Catalog		
Price list		
Brochure		
Business card		
Other		

STEP 4: Merchandise at Your Booth

Accomplishments

In this step you'll:

☐ 1. Learn how to decide what products (or other items) to display in your booth

☐ 2. Get tips and guidelines for displaying the items you take to the show

☐ 3. Discover how to use giveaways and other promotions to turn booth visitors into customers

Time-Saving Tools

You'll complete this step more quickly if you have the following handy:

☐ 1. Your product list and catalog

☐ 2. The "Trade Show Goals" worksheet you completed in Step 1

☐ 3. The "Pre-Show Promotion Plan" you completed in Step 3

Step 4: Merchandise at Your Booth

Just like retailers, trade show exhibitors face the challenge of effective merchandising. Instead of choosing what to display in your store's front window or which items to mark down for a clearance sale, you must decide which products to feature in your booth and whether or not to offer show specials.

You want to attract attendees to your booth, and ideally, convert them into leads. The items you choose to merchandise and the way you display and promote them in your trade show booth will affect the numbers you attract. Giveaways will also attract crowds, but it's important to select items that work within your overall show plan to help you reach your objectives. (For example, unless you're a candy company, handing out free gum for everyone is generous but hardly strategic.)

In order to make your merchandising and in-booth promotion plan succeed, keep the retailer comparison in mind. Think of your booth as a store in a mall crowded with shoppers. How are you going to get them inside to see your products?

The answer to that question includes:

- Knowing what to display
- Knowing how to display it
- Knowing how to promote your booth and products at the show through giveaways, demos, and specials

QUICK**TIP**

Your Most Important Asset

No matter what you choose to display in your booth, the most important item you can take to a trade show is yourself. In the end, new customers will choose to do business with you because of the relationship you build with them, not because you figured out a clever way to display your newest products. Dress and behave as if you're selling yourself—because you are!

QUICK**TIP**

Close at Hand

One way to keep your exhibit focused without losing the opportunity to show curious attendees products not on display is to stash other items under your table. They'll be at hand if you need them, but won't clutter up your booth in the meantime.

1. What to display

What you display in your trade show booth depends on:

- Your trade show goals
- How many products you have
- Whether you're promoting a product or a service

Your Goals

The items you choose to display in your trade show booth should reflect the goals you established for the show as a whole (see Step 1 for guidelines on setting goals).

GOAL	WHAT TO DISPLAY
Generate new leads	Products with the most direct appeal to your target market.
Launch a new product	The product in question, with little else to distract from it.
Increase brand awareness/ raise company visibility	Your highest-profile, best-selling products plus booth graphics featuring your logo prominently.
Meet others in the industry	Your highest-profile products, plus a list of existing customers, and testimonials from some prominent existing customers. New contacts will be more likely to want to meet you if they see notable names on your client list.
Reinforce existing relationships	Your bestsellers. Your current clients will feel validated if they see the products they already use on display.

Your Products

For attendees, one of the advantages of attending a trade show is having the chance to see and touch and try things out. So if your company has physical products, take samples. If they're too big to fit in your booth, take detailed photos and specs.

But which products should you take? If you have only one or two key products, take all of them. If your company has many products, choosing which ones to display can be more challenging. There's no limit on the number of products you can display, but your booth should never feel crowded or look like a garage sale.

Prioritize by asking:

- **What's new?** New products are big attention grabbers, and many exhibitors attend trade shows for the sole purpose of launching new products.
- **What sells best?** If you don't have new products to take or if your new items aren't particularly splashy, round out your display with a few of your most popular items. Your current customers like them, so chances are new ones will, too.
- **What benefits attendees most?** If you sell a wide range of products, take the ones that are most likely to be of interest to your target market.

The more focused you are, the more you can stick to your core selling message. Not only does having too much in your booth look messy, but it dilutes your message. If you want attendees to be able to browse your full product line, take catalogs for them to leaf through.

Even if you're exhibiting at a show where you're expecting to take orders for a line (or multiple lines) of products, keep things streamlined. Attendees need to be able to see at a glance what you sell and decide quickly whether your booth is worth their time.

QUICK**TIP**

Photo Ops

Is your large product line making it difficult for you to decide what to take to the show? Take a picture! Integrating a large photo of your products into your booth—a bookshelf filled with your books or a grocery store shelf stocked with your breakfast cereals—can be more practical (and neater looking) than displaying lots of samples. Even if you have only a few products, integrating visuals of them into your display is a good idea. But remember: every time you update your product line, you'll have to order new photos.

What If You're Selling a Service?

Not all businesses exhibiting at trade shows have products to display. If your company sells a service (hard drive repair, travel bookings, retail construction), focus on showing off your accomplishments instead:

- Put together a binder, computer presentation, or report on past projects. Include photos of completed jobs (if appropriate) and testimonials from satisfied customers.
- Use a list of existing customers as one of your booth graphics. New clients will be influenced if you have a list of notable names on display.
- Use a photo of a product related to your service as a booth graphic. If you offer hard drive repair, this could be a photo of a computer. If you sell travel services, it could show an airplane.

Staying Organized in the Booth

No matter what you choose to display in your exhibit, keep visible clutter to a minimum by:

- **Using space wisely.** If you have a draped table in your booth, store extra supplies and samples out of sight. Make sure that items you hide under the table do not edge out or get kicked out into the aisle where attendees can see them.
- **Improvising.** If you store boxes under a table, make sure the one holding frequently used items (stapler, scissors, and tape, for instance) is accessible.
- **Making order out of chaos.** The best way to keep things tidy is to contain them. If you're going to offer pens for attendees to use, keep them in a holder. If you have several types of printed material on display, corral them all in a neat rack. If you have electrical cords running across the floor, tape them down as discreetly as possible.
- **Leaving as many things as possible in your room.** Take only a wallet with your ID, a credit card, and some cash to the booth.

2. How to display it

A cluttered exhibit is a big turn-off for attendees. Having some empty space in your booth gives their eyes a rest and directs their attention to what's most important. Keeping your display clean and lean focuses attention on your products and core message.

When planning your display:

- **Think in 3-D.** Never arrange your products (or promotional material or past-projects binder) so that they're lying flat. No one will be able to see them from the aisles. Use racks or easels to prop items up. Even if all you have to display is a piece of paper, mount it on foam backing and put it on an easel (available at art supply stores).
- **Mix it up.** Vary the placement of products and other items. If you're displaying several books, arrange some spine-out in stacks and others facing forward. This makes your display more interesting and, if you don't have a lot of products, may give the appearance of a more robust inventory.
- **Be coy.** If you're arranging your products on top of a table, consider positioning the table along the side of your booth, rather than facing the front. This means attendees will need to go into your booth to see what you've got on display. But make sure at least one of the items on the table is facing the aisle so attendees can see *something* as they pass by.
- **Keep a work area open.** If you're going to be asking attendees to fill out lead forms or order forms, make sure there's an open spot they can use as a work area.
- **Make your exhibit space inviting.** Don't put your table next to the aisle. That creates a barrier between you and passing attendees. Arrange your space so attendees can enter your booth easily, even if they come only a few feet in from the aisle.

Dress for Trade Show Success

Trade show dress-code philosophies generally fall into one of four categories:

- **Dress up.** Many show veterans believe that, since you never get a second chance to make a first impression, exhibitors should always wear professional attire: suits, ties, nice dresses.
- **Dress a notch up.** The idea here is to gauge what you think attendees will be wearing and then choose to either match or slightly outdress them. If you think most attendees will be wearing casual pants and jeans, you might choose to wear tailored slacks or a skirt.
- **Dress with your company's logo.** Logo wear is consistent with your branding message and helps reinforce your company identity.
- **Dress in costume.** Some companies have staffers dress in eye-catching or themed costumes to help bring attendees into the booth. This isn't practical when you're running an exhibit by yourself, since you need to be in the booth to answer questions, not roaming the aisles luring attendees to your display.

Your wardrobe represents the culture and values of your company. Remember: what you wear in the booth should fit into your overall promotion and merchandising plan. If you run an upscale limo rental company, it would be jarring if you wore a Hawaiian shirt and linen pants. But if your company made flip flops, that outfit would be completely appropriate.

3. How to promote your products

Attendees are much more likely to include your booth on their agenda if they know ahead of time that you'll be exhibiting. Similarly, attendees are much more likely to visit your booth *during* the show if you do additional promotion while you're there. Options like event sponsorship aren't always realistic for small businesses, but there are several other ways you can boost booth attendance during a show or conference:

- Giveaways
- Demonstrations
- Show specials

Giveaways

Most exhibitors offer attendees a small token during the show—a pen, a pin, a keychain—but the smart ones incorporate memorable giveaways into their promotion plan.

What works:

- **Something tied into your company identity or marketing plan.** Your giveaway items should remind attendees of your message. For example, when the Trade Show Exhibitors Association's tagline was "See the Light," they gave out flashlights. Make sure that any giveaway has your logo (and contact information) imprinted on it.
- **Something useful.** Ideally, whatever you give attendees should be something they'll use and keep on top of their desks. The more they use it, the more frequently they'll see your logo.
- **Different items for different people.** A tiered system of giveaways allows you to give something to everyone, while at the same time reserving the "good stuff" for the really qualified leads. Pens featuring your logo might do for those who expect goodies from every booth. But keep a stash of nicer items hidden away under your table for qualified leads.
- **Something that drives booth visits.** If your main show goal is to get plenty of booth traffic (to build an industry mailing list, for examaple), tie your giveaway to booth attendance. Choose one or two big-ticket items (a DVD player, an iPod) and hold a contest or raffle to give them away. Or hand out something very visible that will make other attendees ask, "Where did you get that?"

What doesn't work:

- **Food items.** Unless your company produces something edible, giving away candy or other food items is a waste of your trade show dollars. Sure, attendees will stop by to grab some, but they're probably coming for a bite to eat, not because they're interested in your product. What's more, edible giveaways have a very short shelf life. Once they're eaten, they're gone, with nothing left to remind the attendee who they came from or what you do. If your company *does* produce edible products, though, having samples in your booth is a necessity.

- **Stuff for kids.** Yes, attendees will line up in front of booths that are giving away stuffed animals or yo-yos, but where do all of those things go the minute they get home? Reduce the chances that your item will end up in the toy box by choosing something meant for grown-ups.

- **Anything corny.** Very few trade show attendees take home everything they collect on the exhibit hall floor. When it's time to pack up and go home, they have to make choices, and the first things to go are often novelty items (mini basketballs, plastic visors) with no practical purpose.

- **Bulky or heavy items.** Unless they're valuable, heavy, hard-to-pack items also end up on the leave-behind list. One business owner gave away mugs for years—until he saw a collection of them on the hotel cleaning cart the day he checked out.

Demonstrations

Demonstrations are a great way to engage attention and educate attendees about your product or service. Almost everyone remembers something better when they've seen it in action—especially if they drive that action themselves.

Demos can range from large group presentations to one-on-one tutorials. But whether your demonstration is large or small, physical (using a product sample to show how it works) or virtual (sharing information on a laptop), it should:

- **Be interactive.** Attendees are more likely to stay for a demonstration if they can participate. If you're talking to a group, ask volunteers to try out a product. If you don't have a product sample in the booth, integrate trivia or other game elements into your computer or DVD presentation to draw attendees' interest.
- **Be brief.** Demos often fail because they're too long or so packed with information that attendees get bored. Make sure your demo is no more than 5 to 7 minutes long—long enough to get your message across, but not so long that anyone's eyes glaze over.
- **Focus on attendees' needs.** Your demo should emphasize the benefits of your product or service, not go into detail about how big it is, how many parts it has, or how long it took to develop.
- **Be personalized.** If you're using a physical product for your demonstration, tailor what you tell each attendee to meet their specific needs. It's harder to personalize a PowerPoint presentation that's been loaded onto a laptop, so if you're walking an attendee through your product one-on-one, opt for natural, give-and-take conversation over a canned pitch.
- **Include a payoff.** Offer a reward —a small giveaway, for example—to attendees who participate and/or stay till the end. People will do just about anything for a desirable prize.
- **Tie in to your giveaway.** If you can use your product to produce a low-cost giveaway, it's a great way to tie everything together. One company that was showing off a new printer set up a machine in their booth for attendees to try, and each demo churned out a customized coaster.

Running a demo in your booth gets attendees involved with your product or service. Those who ask more questions after the demo are likely to be qualified leads—the kind who can give your company more business.

QUICK**TIP**

Easy as Pie

One of the many benefits of an interactive product demonstration is the opportunity to show attendees how easy your product is to use. If you're selling a software program, a food slicer, or a new kind of glue, recruit one booth visitor to try it out while others watch. As long as you've made sure they can complete the demo quickly and easily, you're likely to have a group of converts on your hands.

Show Specials

Many companies that plan to take orders at a show or conference use show-only discounts and other specials as incentives. Typical offers include:

- A percentage off all products ordered during the show
- A percentage off all products *paid for* during the show
- A percentage off all products or services ordered within a certain time period after the show (up to a month, for example)

This tactic can certainly be effective—who doesn't love a good deal?—but it can also backfire. Some buyers, rather than placing orders throughout the year at regular prices, will wait for you to appear at a show so they can get everything for less.

Think carefully before implementing a show-only special. If you act strategically, you can draw in customers *and* protect your bottom line. Consider offering a discount on subsequent orders, rather than the one placed at the show. That way buyers will be motivated to continue working with you. Or use the lure of pre-order access to an upcoming product to drive orders for current products at the show.

Go Guerrilla

Almost any non-traditional promotion idea falls into the "guerrilla" category, meaning that your only limitation (aside from your budget) is your imagination.

The most effective guerrilla promotion tactics are:

- **Creative.** Even the most jaded trade show attendees can be drawn in by a fresh take on an old concept. For example, at the annual Electronic Entertainment Expo (E3), attendees are used to seeing scantily dressed "booth babes" promoting video games. One year, some scruffy guys from a small company put women's underwear on top of their clothes and handed out giveaways, calling themselves the "anti–booth babes."
- **Buzz-worthy.** A few years ago, iOmega handed out buttons with exceptionally clever slogans. Show attendees *wanted* to wear them—effectively becoming walking ads and driving traffic to the iOmega booth. If your goal is to get people to your booth, give away something that attracts notice.
- **Targeted.** If you limit your promotion to a few key players, you can afford to make it memorable. Send your top 5 to 10 leads an empty Mont Blanc pen box before the show and include a note saying they can pick up the pen when they stop by your booth.
- **Daring.** One young entrepreneur went to a big trade show without a booth. After identifying the four top-level executives attending the show he wanted to meet, he convinced each of them to accept a free limo ride from their hotel to the convention center. He got 15 uninterrupted minutes with each of them, and they were impressed with his creativity and tenacity.

QUICK**TIP**

Presentation as Promotion

If you're an industry expert (or someone else in your company is), talk to show management about opportunities to give a talk or make a presentation at the show. This is a particularly appealing option at an academic or association conference, where seminars are frequent and well attended. Giving a good presentation boosts your reputation and also gives your company and your booth greater visibility.

Merchandising Plan

Use this worksheet to summarize your merchandising and promotion plans.

What you'll display:

How you'll display it:

Promotion ideas (include giveaways, demonstrations, and show specials):

STEP 5: Turn Browsers into Buyers

Accomplishments

In this step you'll:

☐ 1. Learn the difference between contacts, prospects, and leads

☐ 2. Learn how to qualify leads

Time-Saving Tools

You'll complete this step more quickly if you have the following handy:

☐ 1. The "Target Customer Profile" worksheet you completed in Step 1

☐ 2. The "Potential Target Customers" worksheet you completed in Step 1

Step 5: Turn Browsers into Buyers

Companies exhibit at trade shows and conferences for many reasons. The most important is to gather leads—that is, the names and contact information of potential customers. This is not surprising, considering that new business from even one solid lead can justify your entire show investment.

But hundreds of people will pass by your exhibit. How can you tell which ones might be good leads? First, you can identify and contact some of them before the show even begins (see Step 3 for details on pre-show contact and promotion).

But you can also qualify leads (decide whether they are potential customers) right on the show floor. How can you do this? Develop a set of questions that allows you to determine quickly whether an attendee fits your target customer profile. And when you've finished the questions, ask the qualified leads for their contact information and agree on a next step to take after the show is over.

To cultivate customers on the exhibition floor:

- Identify leads
- Quickly qualify leads
- Collect information from qualified leads
- Agree on a next step with your qualified leads

QUICK**TIP**

Quality, not Quantity

When you're at a trade show, it's tempting to measure success by the number of business cards you collect. But consider this: If you put out a basket and ask people to drop their card in to win a flat-screen TV, you may very well collect hundreds or even thousands of new names ... but all you really know about them is that they'd love to own a flat-screen TV. Meanwhile, five minutes spent talking to just one truly qualified attendee could result in thousands of dollars of new business. In the world of trade show leads, quality, not quantity, is king.

QUICK**TIP**

Leads by the Numbers

To come up with a rough estimate of the total number of qualified leads you can expect at a given show, complete the following equation:

Net show attendance (total show attendance minus the estimated number of non-buying attendees, which includes exhibitors, press, and so on)

____

x

Percentage of attendees who will be interested in your product or service (estimate 16%–20% for large shows, according to the Center for Exhibition Industry Research)

____

=

Estimated number of qualified leads

____

1. Identify leads

It's a fact of trade show life that not every attendee on the exhibition floor is going to be interested in what you're selling. In fact, the Center for Exhibition Industry Research estimates that on average, only 16% to 20% of a given show's attendees will fall into the "interested" category for any individual exhibitor. That's only one in every four or five of the people who walk by your booth during the show.

That doesn't mean you can forget about the other four people. Most trade show attendees fall into one of these three categories. All are valuable.

- **Contacts.** A contact is anyone you meet who's involved in your industry. You likely don't know much about them except their name and company—in other words, the information on their business cards. If you're looking to expand an industry mailing list or do some networking, contacts are useful.
- **Prospects.** A prospect is a contact who fits your target customer profile (see page 19). You can identify prospects before the show through research or at the show through a qualifying conversation. Because prospects match your definition of a potential customer, they could turn into leads.
- **Leads.** A lead is a prospect who agrees to a specific post-show follow-up action. That action might be a phone call from you, an in-person meeting, an order placement, or even a catalog mailing. The important thing is, they're someone you've talked to, identified as a potential customer, and made concrete plans to contact again after the show.

You will also encounter a certain number of what those in the industry refer to as "adult trick-or-treaters." Usually spouses or other non-industry attendees who tag along to a show with someone else, they cruise the exhibition floor looking for freebies. If someone in this group engages you in a conversation, do your best to end it gracefully but quickly. You need to reserve your time for real leads.

Figuring out who the potential prospects are can be tricky. You may be able to garner some basic information from what's visible on their badge—their name, their company name. But this will probably not be enough to tell whether or not they're a potential lead. That's where the qualification process comes in.

Booth Visit Breakdown

Up to 75% of all attendees have an exhibition floor agenda before they arrive at the show, but plenty of visits are spontaneous.

Top reasons for planned visits:

- Prospects are intrigued by your pre-show promotion plan.
- Attendees saw your name in the list of exhibitors and want to know more about your product or service.
- Industry professionals want to compare your products/services/deals with the competition's.
- Existing customers want to reinforce their relationship with you.

Top reasons for spontaneous visits:

- You engaged them in conversation as they walked by.
- Your booth caught their eye as they walked down the aisle.
- You have a particularly attractive in-booth promotion (a good giveaway, for example, or a flashy demo).
- Other attendees are talking about your company/product/service/booth.

2. Qualify leads

Most show attendees don't make a beeline for your booth, spontaneously provide all the details about who they are and what they do, and announce their intention to place a big order the week after the show. So the only surefire way to tell if someone is a qualified lead with money-making potential is to engage them in conversation and ask them relevant, pointed questions.

Think of each conversation as a five-step process:

1. Make contact
2. Initiate the conversation
3. Direct the conversation
4. Agree on a next step
5. End the conversation

Make Contact

Striking up a conversation with strangers at a trade show can be intimidating. Afraid to be ambushed by exhibitors who are desperate to make a sale, some attendees scurry across the exhibition floor, eyes averted, until they get to the one booth they're interested in. At the same time, some booth staffers, reluctant to make the first move, will hang back inside their exhibits, waiting for the perfect lead to walk up and start asking all the right questions.

Unfortunately, that rarely happens. In order to get the most out of your trade show investment and maximize your qualified leads (which, in turn, maximizes the new business you'll get from the show), you need to be proactive.

But that doesn't mean you have to do a "step right up!" routine like a carnival barker. The best way to start up a conversation with a passing attendee is to make eye contact. If someone avoids your gaze, they're not likely to respond to your opening line either. Another option is to offer them your promotional material or a giveaway, if you have one. If you catch someone's attention, put on your friendliest smile, say hello, and move on to the next phase: initiating the conversation.

Positioned to Succeed

You've rented 100 square feet of exhibit space, set up a beautiful display, and carefully arranged your products. But where do you put yourself?

- **Never stand behind the table.** If you do, it becomes a barrier between you and passing attendees. Pull your table back, leaving room at the front of your exhibit space for attendees to enter. Stand to the side of the table and slightly in front of it.

- **Stand near the front.** There's already enough space between you and the aisle without adding more by standing at the back of your exhibit space. Stand in the front third of the space, close enough to the aisle that you can easily interact with anyone who passes by. Some experts advocate standing with one foot right up on the threshold of your space so you can help "guide" attendees into your booth. But don't be too aggressive; no one wants to feel like they're being attacked when they walk by your exhibit.

- **Stand where it's easy to interact with people.** If you're right-handed, that's probably "stage left" (the front right corner, if you're looking at the booth). Standing in that spot leaves your arms free for hand shaking.

- **Move around.** Standing in one spot for a long time is tiring, and it also makes you appear rigid and inflexible. Changing positions frequently is good for your body and increases your chances of making eye contact with more attendees. But be sure not to pace back and forth.

- **Be realistic.** If you're the only person in the booth for hours on end, you may not be able to stand the whole time. You can talk to people even if you're seated, and it's definitely better to take a chair break with a relaxed, engaging attitude than to stay upright and be tired and cranky.

Model Booth Behavior

Having the right person in your booth can make all the difference when it comes to engaging attendees and qualifying leads. When you have a choice about who to send, opt for someone who:

- **Has extensive product knowledge.** Whoever is in the booth should be able to answer any question about your product or service without hesitation. But that doesn't mean you should send the people who designed or produced your product. Engineers and product managers can get caught up in the complex details of how something works instead of communicating its benefits. Think marketing, not manufacturing.
- **Likes people.** Employees who handle customer service are often good in the booth because they're used to creating relationships quickly and establishing positive connections with strangers.
- **Is warm and outgoing.** Someone who is shy or unapproachable isn't going to be comfortable in a crowd of strangers.
- **Is a good listener.** Booth staffers need to be able to pick up cues from attendees so they know how to direct their conversations to meet attendees' needs.
- **Understands the trade show dynamic.** Making connections at a trade show is different from selling in the field. Someone who has been to shows before and understands how they work is likely to do better than someone who's never attended one.
- **Is healthy and energetic.** Nothing turns people off faster than someone who's sneezing and coughing and/or leaning on the exhibit because they're exhausted or uninterested.
- **Has interacted with your customers before.** Sometimes playing up the "Let's finally put a face to a name!" angle will help draw attendees to your booth.
- **Will be attending shows in the future.** As long as you have someone experienced on hand, send along a newbie for training, too. The only way to become a trade show pro is to get out there and start learning.

Be sure your booth staff follows a few basic rules: No eating, smoking, or gum chewing in the booth and no cell phone conversations or texting. Exceptions can be made to the first rule at mealtime if you're by yourself and to the last if something business-critical comes up.

QUICK**TIP**

The Secret Language of Badges

Many trade shows and conferences give attendees color-coded badges to indicate their function or place within the industry. Knowing in advance which colors to look out for—blue for buyers, for example—can give you a shortcut to qualifying (or disqualifying) leads. Ask show management about what color coding, if any, you can expect to see on the exhibition floor.

Initiate the Conversation

Once you've made eye contact with an attendee, your next job is to start a conversation. Introduce yourself, shake hands, and then start off with an open-ended question that gets attendees to share something about themselves: "How are you enjoying the show?" or "Tell me why you're here today." People love talking about themselves, so you can't go wrong with this line of questioning.

An attendee's badge can also be a great source of ice-breaker conversation. Read it to see where they're from. If it's some distance away, sympathize with how far they've had to travel: "It must be nice to be here at last after flying such a long way!" Or if you've been there, kick-start a rapport by sharing your experiences: "I see you're from Chicago. I had the best pizza there last year!" Make sure your comments are not too personal. Keep the banter light, and be open to changing direction or letting the attendee move on if you see you are not getting a positive response.

When you're getting a conversation started, engaging the attendee matters more than the specific content of your questions. Be frank and open, rather than contrived or "salesy." People can spot a canned pitch a mile off, and they'll respond more positively to someone who sounds sincerely interested in who they are and what they need.

What's My Line?

When it comes to starting a conversation, it's hard to beat a friendly "hello." But what should you say after that? Opt for open-ended questions. Rather than asking, "Are you enjoying the show?" try "How's the show going?" Other good openers:

- "What brings you to the show today?"
- "How are you enjoying the show?"
- "What are you looking for at the show today?"

Then, a bit later in the conversation, you could ask:

- "What prompted you to visit our exhibit today?"
- "Tell me what issues your company is dealing with right now."

Direct the Conversation

Once you're past the ice-breaker phase, start talking business as soon as possible. To maximize your potential for generating new business, you want to speak with as many potential leads as possible, so aim to spend no more than five minutes per conversation. Attendees want to visit as many exhibits as they can, so it's in everyone's interest to get to the point.

Your list of qualifying questions should be designed to help you figure out whether the person you're speaking with meets your target customer profile. When you're coming up with your list, work backwards: Think about your best current customers and which questions you'd have asked them when you first met to decide if they were a good fit.

Qualifying questions can cover the following topics:

TOPIC	WHY YOU WANT TO ASK ABOUT IT
What company does the attendee work for?	To find out if it's a company you've heard of and would like to do business with and/or if it's a company within your section of the industry.
What needs does the attendee's company currently have?	To find out how your product or service can help, so you can emphasize its most relevant benefits.
How is the attendee's company currently meeting those needs?	To find out which, if any, of your competitors the attendee's company is currently doing business with. This gives you the chance to talk about your product or service's benefits from a competitive-advantage standpoint.
What role does the attendee have at their company?	To find out if they have the power to decide whether or not to do business with you.
How quickly is the attendee looking to make a decision/change?	To find out what kind of timeline the attendee has. This will help you focus your post-show follow-up. If they're ready to act immediately, you can be more aggressive than if they're not planning to make immediate changes.
What kind of budget is the attendee working with?	To help you assess how valuable the attendee could be as a customer.

Of course, you're not going to make it through all of these topics with each person you talk to. You may find out, for instance, that their company doesn't really need your product or service. In that case, you'd politely end the conversation. But you may decide, after the course of your initial qualifying questions, that the prospect you're speaking to *does* match your target customer profile and could be a solid lead. In that case, you can collect their contact information and agree on a next step.

Qualifying Questions

Use this worksheet to create questions you can ask trade show attendees to discover whether they meet your target customer profile.

1.

2.

3.

4.

5.

6.

7.

Information, Please

To streamline the qualification process, you can ask prospects to complete a lead form—a card or piece of paper used to collect information on qualified attendees. This technique works well at smaller shows, where you have more time to spend with each booth visitor. At larger shows, you can jot down this information yourself in a notebook reserved for that purpose.

Lead forms typically ask for:

- **Contact information.** Name, company, title, business address, phone and fax numbers, email address. To save time, staple prospects' business cards to your forms (or into your notebook).
- **Some basic facts about their business and its needs.** Ask whatever you need to know to decide whether a prospect fits your target customer profile and to determine how to follow up with them after the show.
- **Trade show name and date, plus booth staffer's name.** If you're attending multiple shows, you want to be able to tell which leads came from each one.

Lead forms are helpful for several reasons:

- They provide a record of all the prospects you spoke to.
- They help ensure that you don't forget to ask a critical question.
- They allow you to rank prospects while their name and information are fresh in your mind. Noting a quick A, B, or C (or 1, 2, or 3) on a form will help you prioritize the hottest leads when you're back in the office.
- You can offer promotional items only to the attendees who fill out a form. (This helps keep your giveaways out of the hands of adult trick-or-treaters.)

You can complete the lead form with a prospect in an interview-like process or you can ask the prospect to fill it out on their own. If you let a prospect fill the form out on their own, you can initiate a conversation with another attendee.

However, if you start talking with someone else, you may not be able to gracefully end the first conversation. You might miss the opportunity of establishing a relationship that could lead to solid business. You may also lose the chance to make notes on the form while the details of your interaction are still fresh in your mind. For those reasons, when circumstances allow, go with the interview approach.

Some companies opt for electronic versions of the lead form. Exhibitors can buy or rent business-card scanners and computer-based lead retrieval systems. These options definitely have a certain "cool" factor, and having your lead information computerized is handy. But is the extra expense worth it? It's the information that matters, not how you collect it. As long as you get the information you need from a prospect, it makes no difference how you get it.

Treat completed lead forms, or your lead-filled notebook, like gold: Keep them safe, keep them with you, and *don't* ship them home with your other show materials! Pack them in your carry-on luggage. If a shipment gets lost or delayed, so will your ability to follow up with the leads you've collected.

Agree on a Next Step

A trade show attendee becomes a lead only when the two of you agree on a next step to take after the show. That step can be small or large, but before the lead leaves your booth, both of you must know that you'll be in touch again soon and for a specific reason.

Possible next steps include:

- Placing an order
- Scheduling an in-person sales call or meeting
- Scheduling a phone call
- Sending a sample product
- Mailing a catalog (or other marketing/promotional material)
- Sending a follow-up email

The best time to transition into "next step" mode is after you've explained to the lead how your product or service can help fill their company's needs. Assuming the lead responds positively, suggest a follow-up: "I'd appreciate the opportunity to go over all of this in more detail. Can I call you next week?"

The more you can get a lead to commit to, the better. If they agree to a meeting or phone call, try to set a specific date and time. (Many people don't have their calendars with them on the show floor, but it doesn't hurt to try.) Then follow through on whatever you promise to do. If you say you'll call, call. If you say you'll send a sample product or a catalog, send it. (See Step 8 for more details on post-show follow-up.)

Think Globally

Many large trade shows and conferences attract attendees from around the world, so it's important to be aware of potential cultural differences.

When interacting with international attendees:

- **Keep humor to a minimum.** Jokes rarely travel well. In the same vein, avoid slang whenever possible. Use straightforward business terms.
- **Don't raise your voice.** If someone doesn't speak English, talking louder won't make them understand you. Try speaking more slowly instead.
- **Take your time.** The five-minute conversation rule can be bent for international prospects, who are probably used to taking more time to establish new relationships, often over meals, drinks, or other hospitality events. If someone from another country seems like a particularly strong lead, offer to meet them after the show closes for the day, when you have more time for a leisurely discussion.
- **Be polite and respectful.** Don't call international attendees by their first names without permission. Extend your respect to the attendees' business cards. Treat them carefully, and don't fold them or scribble notes on the back.
- **Think before shaking.** Not everyone greets with a handshake. Europeans typically do, but many Asians prefer a nod or a bow.

End the Conversation

When in doubt about how to end a conversation, be honest and frank. Said in a friendly tone, "It's been great talking to you, but I see some other people waiting" is unlikely to upset anyone. Accompany the line with a second handshake.

Your closing approach will differ depending on who you're talking to:

- **A qualified lead.** Once you've agreed on that crucial next step, your conversation with a qualified lead will end naturally: "Thanks for coming by. I'll see/call/email you next week." If a lead shows signs of impatience in the middle of your conversation, make sure you've secured their contact information, then wrap things up.
- **A contact.** Your conversation with a contact will probably end sooner than a conversation with a qualified lead. Once you've determined that they aren't ready to move into the prospect category, take their card and offer a second handshake.
- **Neither of the above.** When you get caught talking to someone who isn't a contact, a prospect, *or* a lead, you need to end the conversation as quickly and gracefully as possible: "It sounds like you have a great company, but I don't think our product is really what you're looking for right now." You can also try the "It's been great talking to you, but..." approach, ending with whatever makes sense: "... I see some other people waiting," "... I have to take care of [add what you need to take care of]," or "... I need to grab a stack of fresh catalogs."

You can combine your closing with a low-ticket giveaway item. If you have pens printed with your company's logo, for example, you can offer a pen and a handshake and say: "We've been giving all our booth visitors a pen on their way out today to say thanks for coming by."

QUICK**TIP**

Be Shoe Savvy

If you can't escape the show floor for more than a few minutes, one fast, easy way to re-energize is to change your shoes. Be sure to take at least two pairs of comfortable, broken-in shoes with you, ideally with slightly different heel heights. Switching between pairs will automatically change your posture and make your feet feel better.

Other helpful conversation closers:

- "I hope that's answered all of your questions. If not, please feel free to follow up next week." (Make sure to hand over one of your business cards if you use this line.)
- "Those sessions must be keeping you really busy. I don't want to take up all of your time on the floor."
- "There's a lot more information on our company website; do you have the URL?" (Then give it to them and send them on their way.)

You're likely to find yourself talking to people who just won't take a hint. If potentially qualified leads are lining up, you need to be free to talk to them. Without being rude, do whatever you need to do to end the conversation. Apologize ("I'm so sorry. I've really enjoyed our conversation, but someone else is waiting"), smile, and move away. This is the strongest signal you can send that it's over.

Re-energizing the Booth-Bound

Spending hours on your feet in an exhibition hall and having conversations with strangers all day long is physically and mentally exhausting. So take some time for yourself. If there are any scheduled breaks or a night without a social event, do something to get your mind off the show, whether it's having a nice dinner or going to a movie. No one expects you to work for 10 hours straight in the office without taking a break, and a trade show is no different.

Don't feel guilty about indulging yourself during your free time. Order room service. Get a massage. Keeping your energy levels up while you're in the booth may require a little pampering when you're not.

Going It Alone

Going to a trade show or conference by yourself can be challenging, but there are ways to make solo shows more manageable:

- **Know your neighbors.** Make friends with the exhibitors next to and across from you. If you need to go to the bathroom or grab a snack, they can keep an eye on your booth.
- **Ask for help.** Even if you can put up and dismantle your exhibit by yourself, an extra pair of hands can make a huge difference. Recruit one of your neighbors and offer to return the favor.
- **Stock up.** Make sure you have all the materials you'll need during the day: pens, catalogs, business cards. Store extras under your table in case you run out in the middle of the day.
- **Plan ahead.** You'll need meal and bathroom breaks, but you can minimize their impact on your time in the booth by planning ahead. Eat a big breakfast and hit the facilities before you arrive at the booth.
- **Eat.** You need food to maintain your energy and water to stay hydrated. Keep meals and snacks discreet and easy to manage (granola bars, bottled water, small sandwiches). Try to eat them during slow periods. Remember to take breath mints and lozenges to keep your throat in good condition.
- **Sit down.** Try to take your chair breaks when traffic is light, but don't force yourself to stay on your feet even in high-traffic times.
- **Get moving.** Working in a booth for eight hours is exhausting. When traffic is slow, go for brisk walks up and down your aisle to keep your energy level up. (But always keep your exhibit in sight.)
- **Take a break.** Study the exhibition hall schedule so you can plan breaks for times when most attendees will be in sessions or at meals. If your neighbors can't watch your booth, spread a tablecloth over anything you think might disappear while you're gone.
- **Be welcoming.** Acknowledge everyone who comes into your booth, even if you're talking to someone else. If you can, include the newcomer in your existing conversation: Voila! You've turned a one-on-one chat into a mini-presentation.
- **Take audioisual aids.** You may not be able to break away from all conversations to acknowledge a new booth visitor. So you should have something else in the booth to capture their attention: a computer presentation, for example, or a portfolio of past projects.
- **Keep it simple.** If you know you're going to be attending most or all of your company's trade shows and conferences by yourself, make sure your exhibit is easy to operate.

STEP 6: Think Outside the Booth

Accomplishments

In this step you'll:

☐ 1. Learn how to make the most of meetings with customers and contacts

☐ 2. Discover how to use meals to create business relationships

☐ 3. Learn what you can find out by observing the competition

Time-Saving Tools

You'll complete this step more quickly if you have the following handy:

☐ The "Potential Target Customers" worksheet you completed in Step 1

☐ The daily schedule for the show you're planning to attend

Step 6:
Think Outside the Booth

You won't spend all your time in your booth at a trade show or conference. At many association and academic conferences, the exhibition hall is open for only a few hours between seminar sessions, and even the most exhibit-focused trade shows have to close at the end of the day. There will be times during exhibit hours when you need to take a break.

So how do you make the most of time spent outside the booth? If you're on the show floor, you can scope out the competition, get ideas for future shows, and maybe even meet a few new leads. When the exhibition hall is closed, you can take current or potential customers and partners out for coffee or out on the town.

The important thing is to make a conscious decision about your time out of the booth and plan how to use it to help meet your overall show goals. Exhibiting at a trade show is a big investment; using your time wisely will help you get the maximum return.

QUICK**TIP**

No Booth? No Problem!

You don't have to have a booth at a trade show to accomplish your show goals. Going to a show as an attendee allows you to walk the exhibition floor at your leisure and gives you flexibility in making appointments with existing and potential clients. Do your homework before the show to research leads and set meetings with them so you can use your time profitably at the show.

QUICK**TIP**

Guerrilla Appointment Setting

While it's usually more efficient (and less stressful) to line up appointments with clients and contacts before a show begins, it is possible to do it while the show is underway. Keep your eyes and ears open at all times for chances to schedule meetings with existing customers or potential leads. Opportunity could strike in the elevator, at events, or even walking around the hotel.

1. Meet with current clients and contacts off the floor

While most companies go to trade shows with the goal of generating new customer leads, it's important to pay attention to your current clients and contacts as well. If they're happy with your relationship, repeat business will keep on coming. They may connect you with new leads as well, if they recommend you to colleagues and friends. And if you have new products, you need to sell them to your existing customers, too.

As part of your pre-show promotion plan (see Step 3), you've already found out what current customers and contacts are going to be at the show. The next step is to contact them to set up appointments. Making arrangements before the show is key, since it will be much more difficult to track them down during the show.

These appointments can either be for specific times to come by the booth or for times that don't overlap with regular booth hours. One advantage of meeting outside the booth is that you won't be interrupted by other attendees. Work around exhibition hall hours and set meetings for breakfast, dinner, or other times when the floor is closed. (See pages 101-102 for tips on successful business meals.)

QUICK**TIP**

Go Undercover

If you're at a show where most of your products are displayed on a table, rather than on racks or stands, and you have to leave your booth to take a break, cover your table with a plain cloth. If they're hidden, your products and other equipment will be much less likely to disappear while you're gone. Try to do this only while floor traffic is slow. Otherwise, passing attendees won't see any of the items you have on display.

If your budget allows, invite your best current customers to join you on a special outing. Take them to the theater or treat them to a round of golf the Sunday after the show. If the trade show is in a destination city such as New York, Chicago, or Las Vegas, your customers will think of the show as a mini-vacation. So they'll leap at the chance to relax and have fun. If necessary, arrive a day early or stay a day late to accommodate your customers' schedules.

When you're at meals, meetings, or other excursions, your first priority is to reinforce your existing relationship with your customers. You don't have to be all business, all the time. In fact, when you're at a social event, it's better to chat about things completely unrelated to the show or your industry. People do business with people they like, and getting to know your customers as people is an essential part of establishing a lasting rapport. (However, you should be prepared to talk details in case your customer is ready and willing to place an order or make a deal.)

Networking Basics

Brush up on your networking skills before attending a trade show:

- **Take business cards.** Hand a business card over as you introduce yourself. If you don't get one in return, feel free to ask for one. If the person doesn't have a card, jot down their contact information on the back of one of your own cards or in your trade show notebook.

- **Wear a name tag or badge.** This helps people remember your name as well as your company's name.

- **Approach people.** Start by talking to people in the drinks line or next to the buffet table. At business events, it's perfectly appropriate to start a conversation with "Hi, I'm ..." or to make a positive comment about the food or the room. You don't have to be clever. The point is to start a conversation.

- **Have your "elevator pitch" ready.** An elevator pitch is a brief description of your company that you could give in the time it takes to ride up a few floors on an elevator. It should clearly and concisely convey the core aspects of your business.

- **Actively listen.** Ask other people questions and then really listen to their answers. Use your time to establish rapport rather than trying to make a sales pitch.

- **Move on.** Mingling means moving around. So don't stay with the same people for the whole event. You can excuse yourself to go to get another drink or you can end a conversation with "It's been great talking to you. I'd love to follow up after the show."

2. Make mealtimes into networking times

When you're at a trade show, every show-related activity is an opportunity for networking and relationship building—particularly meals. Show management often plans nightly dinners and receptions, which are great opportunities for catching up with existing clients, making new industry contacts, and discovering a few more potential leads.

If you want to spend quality time with an existing customer or start getting to know a new lead, you can also make breakfast and dinner dates away from the hotel or convention center. (Lunch meetings are usually trickier to arrange, since you'll be on booth duty, and attendees will be busy at sessions or on the exhibition floor.)

Talking to a prospective client over a meal is a great way to establish a warm working relationship. To make a business meal a success:

- **Focus on your relationship.** Business meals provide the perfect opportunity for you and your prospect to get to know each other as people. Establishing common interests makes working together easier.
- **Be an active listener.** The most important things you can do at a business meal are to listen and to ask questions about your guest as a person. Ask about where they grew up, their family, hobbies, and so on. Just try not to make it feel like an interview and keep the personal questions light and general.
- **Don't rush.** There's no need to treat a working meal like a fast-food dinner. Order multiple courses and eat slowly. If your guest is doing most of the talking, they'll have less time than you to eat and may become uncomfortable if you finish first.

QUICK**TIP**

Savvy Socializing

Experienced show managers plan receptions for attendees inside the exhibition hall. These receptions and other events increase booth traffic and give you more chances of meeting new leads. Keep an eye out for this type of reception in your show program and make sure you have someone in your booth while they're underway.

- **Keep it simple.** Avoid potentially messy dishes like pasta and topping-heavy burgers. Your food should require as little attention as possible so you can focus on your guest.
- **Don't drink.** It's never wise to mix business with alcohol. You want to stay alert. Don't order a drink if your guest doesn't, and if you do opt for a beer or a glass of wine, have only one.
- **Hang up.** Turn off your cell phone. If your customer or prospect is important enough to take out for a meal, don't insult them with a ringing phone.
- **Don't take a lot of paperwork.** Unless your customer or lead has asked to see a presentation, catalog, or samples, leave them in your room. If you do take something, put it in your briefcase and put your briefcase on the floor until your guest asks to see it.
- **Pick up the tab.** Unless your guest has a specific objection to being treated (some companies don't allow employees to accept free meals), you should pay for all business meals.

Network with Potential Partners

Trade shows offer you great opportunities to scope out new suppliers, partners, and other complementary businesses. It's rare to have so many companies from the same industry gathered in one place, so take advantage.

Read the exhibitor list before you arrive at the show to identify any particularly good prospects. Consider contacting them before the show to set up appointments, just as you would for a strong customer lead. Even a get-acquainted coffee break could be enough to start a new relationship.

Once you're at the show, keep an eye out for potential allies whenever you're on the exhibition floor. Don't interrupt their booth staffers when they're talking to someone, but engage them in conversation if they're free. Learn what you can about their business and think about how you might work together. Be sure to exchange business cards and suggest trading hot leads. If you promise to refer attendees to them whenever it makes sense, chances are they'll do the same for you.

3. Check out the competition

Spending three days in a big room full of other companies in your industry gives you an excellent opportunity to scope out the competition.

When you can manage to get out of your booth, walk the exhibition floor. You can get up to speed on competitors' latest products and other offerings, and you can assess their trade show approach. Observing your competitors' booths and the way they run them might give you ideas for how to improve or adjust your own approach to exhibiting. Or they might show you what *not* to do!

Pay attention to:

- **Their booths.** How have your competitors displayed their products? What products have they chosen to display? What do their graphics tell you about their business? About their client list? About their products? You don't want your display to look exactly like your competitors', but it's worth noting what elements of their exhibit promote positive reactions from attendees.
- **Their products.** What new products or services have your competitors recently released? What upgrades or new features have they added? How are their products priced?
- **Their staffers.** What is the competition's booth staff wearing? If you have a chance to talk to one of them, note how they engage you in conversation and what they say about their products. Compare this to your own conversations with attendees: Was there anything the competition did better? Worse?
- **Their marketing materials.** Pick up their literature and catalogs if you can. This will give you insights into their product lines, prices, and positioning. What benefits do they promote? What advantages might their products or services have over yours (or vice versa)? You can tailor your own marketing materials to help differentiate your business from theirs.

As long as they're not in the middle of a conversation, don't hesitate to talk to your competitors. They probably already know who you are, and you'll definitely be seeing each other at other shows and conferences, so it's polite to say hello.

In the end, success depends much more on what *you* do than on what your competitors are doing. You can define excellence in your own business without focusing on beating the competition. Don't ignore them, but don't let them dictate how you do business in the office or on the show floor.

Competitor Evaluation

Use this worksheet to evaluate your competitors' trade show presence.

What does their booth look like? (What do the graphics say? What products are on display? How big is the booth?)

What products or services are they offering? (What are the upgrades or features? What is the pricing?)

How successful are their staffers? (What are they wearing? How do they open and close conversations?)

What do their marketing materials accomplish? (What materials do they have on hand in the booth? What information is included? Do they have any giveaways? Special promotions?)

"Outside the Booth" Plan

Use this worksheet to schedule your time on and off the show floor. Pencil in all client/contact appointments, exhibition hall hours (note which times are concurrent with meals or seminars), trade show social events, and any other plans you make.

	DAY ONE	DAY TWO	DAY THREE	DAY FOUR
7 a.m.				
8 a.m.				
9 a.m.				
10 a.m.				
11 a.m.				
Noon				
1 p.m.				
2 p.m.				
3 p.m.				
4 p.m.				
5 p.m.				
6 p.m.				
7 p.m.				
8 p.m.				
9 p.m.				
10 p.m.				
11 p.m.				
Midnight				

NOTES:

7

STEP 1: Choose the Right Show

STEP 2: Book the Show

STEP 3: Create Promotion and Marketing Materials

STEP 4: Merchandise at Your Booth

STEP 5: Turn Browsers into Buyers

STEP 6: Think Outside the Booth

STEP 7: Follow-Up

STEP 8: Evaluate the Show

STEP 9: The Booth

STEP 10: Show Shipments

Accomplishments

In this step you'll:

☐ 1. Learn how to organize the leads and contacts you collected at the show

☐ 2. Get tips on the best ways to follow up with trade show leads and contacts

☐ 3. Find out how to make the most of post-show promotion

Time-Saving Tools

You'll complete this step more quickly if you have the following handy:

☐ All the lead and contact data you collected at the show

☐ Your existing customer/lead/contact database

Step 7: Follow-Up

Following up promptly with the leads you meet at a trade show or conference is essential. If you wait too long, they may forget about your product or service or place an order with a competitor. You could gain an advantage over the competition by sending a simple email or making a phone call.

Start by organizing the lead contact information you collected at the show. Many off-the-shelf computer programs have been designed to help organize contact information. But if you've used a trade show notebook, your lead information should all be in one place.

Even more important than getting organized is getting in touch with the people you met at the show. Act fast and deliver on any and all promises you made to them. If you said you'd call, call. If you said you'd send a catalog, put it in the mail right away. Exhibiting at a trade show is expensive. The sooner you follow up on the contacts you met there, the greater the chances your investment will pay off.

This Step shows you how to:

- Organize the data you collected at the trade show
- Follow up on your leads and contacts
- Do post-show promotion

QUICK**TIP**

Don't Delay

Your job isn't finished when you pack the last box of show supplies and head for the airport. In fact, one of your most important show-related tasks is just beginning: following up on your leads and contacts. Start the follow-up process as soon as you get back to the office.

QUICK**TIP**

Grow Your Mailing List

Add every person you meet at a trade show, from hot lead to industry contact, to your company's mailing list. The people who aren't in the market for your product or service right now may know someone who is. Or they may become buyers themselves in the future.

1. Organize your data

The first step in organizing information you've collected at a trade show is to rank your leads. Record the following information directly on a lead form (see page 89 for more on lead forms), on the back of a lead's business card, or in your trade show notebook:

- Where they fall on whatever scale you choose to use: 1 through 5, A through F, 1 star through 5 stars
- Any additional information that will help you remember the person and your conversation with them ("Wore red sweater," "From San Diego," "Wants to order 200 units")
- Whatever you promised to do after the show: call, email, send a catalog

According to industry sources, up to 80 percent of trade show leads aren't followed up. Don't let your data collect dust. Add all of your new leads and contacts to a customer contact system right away: during downtime at the show, on the plane home, or as soon as you get back to the office. Several customer relationship management (CRM) software programs are available for exactly this purpose. The advantage of using a computerized CRM system is that it puts a uniform, centrally located data repository right at your fingertips. When you're talking to one of your contacts on the phone, it's quick and easy to pull up your entire business relationship history.

QUICK**TIP**

Track Your Customer Contacts

If you invest in customer relationship management software, use it. Log every contact you have with your leads and customers, even if it's just a quick email or phone call. Note the date, the type of contact, and what was discussed or agreed upon.

Organizing Data

These days, most companies use some kind of computer database program to store and maintain contact data. Computerized databases are easy to sort, can be backed up, and usually integrate easily with your accounting software and computer address book.

But there are non-technical options as well:

- Use color-coded file folders to sort your lead data: red for high-priority leads, yellow for medium-priority, and green for low-priority.
- Use paper clips or sticky notes to mark specific items within each file that need a particular type of follow-up.
- Use a Rolodex to keep names and numbers in order.
- Keep individual, dated trade show notebooks and flag the pages containing high-priority contacts and follow-up items.

2. Follow-up

As soon as a show is over, your focus will switch to following up with the leads and contacts you gathered. Your initial post-show contact should take place between one day and one week after the show ends while memories are still fresh. Aim to do your first round of follow-up the first day you get back to your office. Put it at the top of your priority list.

First Contact

The fastest, easiest way to do your first round of follow-up is to send all of your leads an email. It doesn't have to be long or complicated. Thank them for visiting your booth during the show, remind them who you are and what your company does, and if you agreed to take further action, tell them they'll be hearing from you again very soon. Personalize your message and don't be too vague in your subject line. You don't want the recipient to think your message is spam.

Sample follow-up email

From: *YOUR NAME*

To: *LEAD OR CONTACT NAME*

Subject: *TRADE SHOW NAME follow-up: Thanks for visiting YOUR COMPANY's booth*

Dear LEAD or CONTACT NAME:

Thank you so much for stopping by our booth at TRADE SHOW NAME in CITY NAME this weekend. It was a pleasure to see you and talk to you about YOUR PRODUCT/SERVICE NAME. I hope you had a safe trip back to HOME TOWN.

Per our discussion, I'll be sending you a copy of our catalog later this week. I'll give you a call next week to make sure it arrived and answer any questions you might have. In the meantime, you can contact me anytime at YOUR EMAIL ADDRESS or YOUR PHONE NUMBER.

Again, thanks very much, and I look forward to speaking with you soon.

Sincerely,

YOUR NAME

YOUR CONTACT INFORMATION

QUICK**TIP**

Follow Your Leads

If your leads have specified a preferred method or time to be contacted, stick to their preferences. The best way to follow up with a lead is the way that lead wants you to.

For your strongest leads, you may want to skip the acknowledgment and go straight to the follow-up, sending a catalog or samples right away. In that case, the first sentence of the second paragraph should be changed to: "*Per our discussion, I've enclosed a copy of our catalog.*" If you have an electronic copy of your catalog, you can send it as an email attachment. If not, send a business letter using the wording shown and enclose the actual catalog. Skip the acknowledgment email only if you have time to send out catalogs *and* contact everyone else within the first day after you've returned from the show.

In emails to leads and contacts with whom you *haven't* agreed on a next step, the second paragraph can be more general:

From: *YOUR NAME*

To: *LEAD OR CONTACT NAME*

Subject: *TRADE SHOW NAME follow-up: Thanks for visiting YOUR COMPANY's booth*

Dear LEAD or CONTACT NAME:

Thank you so much for stopping by our booth at TRADE SHOW NAME in CITY NAME this weekend. It was a pleasure to see you and talk to you about YOUR PRODUCT/SERVICE NAME. I hope you had a safe trip back to HOME TOWN.

Please contact me if you have questions about our company or our products. You can reach me anytime at YOUR EMAIL ADDRESS or YOUR PHONE NUMBER.

Sincerely,

YOUR NAME

YOUR CONTACT INFORMATION

QUICK**TIP**

Short and Sweet

Keep your follow-up correspondence—email or otherwise—short and to the point. Your prospective customers are as busy as you are, and they'll appreciate it if you're direct and concise. If something important won't fit in an email, post it on your company's website and include a link to it in the body of your message instead.

If you have a single-page product highlight sheet, consider attaching it to general emails, but don't send a large file that could tie up the recipient's in-box.

If you have a large number of follow-up emails to send, consider delegating the task to an employee or hiring a temp. As long as your address is in the "from" field, your template is used, and each message is personalized, no one has to know you didn't hit the "send" key yourself.

Subsequent Contact

What happens next depends on the type of lead or contact you're communicating with and what you promised to do. For contacts who aren't currently true leads, there's no need for additional show-specific follow-up. Just keep them on your mailing list for company newsletters and other bulletins.

For real leads—solid customer prospects with whom you agreed on a post-show action during your in-booth conversation—your next step is to fulfill that agreement. If you promised to send a catalog or product samples, send them out within a week of your return from the show. If you said you'd call to take the order they wanted to place, call. If you said you'd make an appointment to see them, schedule it.

Email and Letters

You can use a version of the letter below for the next round of follow-up. Keep it short, personalized, and actionable. Your goal is to move these relationships to the next level.

In emails or letters with materials attached:

From: *YOUR NAME*

To: *LEAD OR CONTACT NAME*

Subject: *TRADE SHOW NAME follow-up: More Information on YOUR COMPANY'*

Dear LEAD OR CONTACT NAME:

I hope things are settling down for you now that TRADE SHOW NAME is over.

Per your request, I've attached a copy of our latest catalog. I look forward to discussing our products with you after you've had a chance to look through it.

I'll give you a call next week to make sure everything arrived and to answer any questions you might have. Please let me know if there's a specific time that works well for you. You can contact me anytime at YOUR EMAIL ADDRESS or YOUR PHONE NUMBER.

Sincerely,

YOUR NAME

YOUR CONTACT INFORMATION

In every follow-up message that you send, don't hesitate to add brief, relevant information about the products you featured in your booth or any specials or sales you're offering.

QUICK**TIP**

Make Contact Easy

Your leads should never have to hunt for a way to reach you. Include your contact information—name, title, company name, mailing address, email address, office phone number, fax, cell phone number, website—in all of your follow-up correspondence. When leaving a voice mail, speak slowly and clearly, spell out your email address, and repeat your phone number.

Phone Calls

Email and letters are helpful tools for making quick post-show contact, but at some point you need to talk to your leads directly if you want to establish a lasting rapport. If your first follow-up (after the general acknowledgement email) is a phone call, plan to make the call a week after the show ends or earlier. Use this script as a starting point:

"Hi, LEAD NAME. This is YOUR NAME from YOUR COMPANY. We spoke the other day at TRADE SHOW NAME, and I'm calling to follow up on our conversation. If you recall, we discussed (INSERT REFERENCE TO TOPICS COVERED IN YOUR TRADE SHOW CONVERSATION, such as "We discussed your search for a new solution for your needs and that you wanted more detail on our product").

What are some of the questions I can answer for you about YOUR PRODUCT? [Answer all questions.]

What else do you need? [Turn this into an action item. Offer to send product samples or a catalog, or to take an order if they're ready. If you promise to send something, do it the same day. Then call again a few days later to follow up.]

Thanks so much for your time. Let me make sure you have my contact information. [Give it to them.]

Please don't hesitate to call or email if you have any questions. Thanks again—and I'll follow up next week. I look forward to working with you."

It's always helpful to have a starting point for business conversations like these, but go with the flow when you're speaking to a lead. The last thing you want to do is sound rehearsed.

If you've already sent samples or materials, call to follow up a few days after you think they've been received (two to three days after sending an email and about a week if sending via post). Use this version of the script:

> "*Hi, LEAD NAME. This is YOUR NAME from YOUR COMPANY. We met the other day at TRADE SHOW NAME, and I'm calling to make sure you received the catalog I sent.*
>
> *Do you have any questions I can answer about YOUR PRODUCT? [Answer all questions.]*
>
> *Is there anything else you need? [Turn this into an action item. Offer to take an order if your lead is ready. If they're not, find out why and address the issue if possible. If you can't take the order—they don't have the budget right now, they need to check with someone else—schedule a follow-up call or an in-person appointment for a convenient time.]*
>
> *Thanks so much for your time. Let me make sure you have my contact information. [Give it to them.]*
>
> *Please don't hesitate to call or e-mail if you have any questions. Thanks again—and I look forward to working with you.*"

Meetings

Sometimes a phone call isn't enough to move things to the next level. Nothing beats "face time" for building and maintaining relationships. If any of your hottest leads seem likely to commit to a big order, you can nudge them toward the dotted line by scheduling an in-person meeting as soon after the show as your schedules allow.

It's more difficult to script an in-person meeting than a phone call, since it's even more important that you not sound rehearsed. But after you and your lead exchange pleasantries, something like this should help get the conversation started:

> "*Thanks so much for taking time to meet with me today. I know you're busy, so we can get right to the point. Are there any questions I can answer about YOUR PRODUCT? [Answer all questions.]*
>
> *Okay, I think that's everything! [Suggest the next step—offer to take an order if they're ready. If they're not, find out why and address the issue if possible. If you can't take an order—they don't have the budget right now, they need to check with someone else—schedule a follow-up call or another appointment.]*"

Don't forget to say thank you and leave your business card as well as any additional product materials you may have.

It's a good idea to schedule in-person appointments with any leads in your area, whether they're top-priority or not. Stop by their office for a meeting or invite them out to lunch or dinner. Use the tips on business meals on pages 101-102 to make the most of your time together.

Know When to Say When

After your acknowledgment email, your first action step, and its subsequent follow-up, refrain from calling or emailing a lead more frequently than every two to three weeks. And unless you're getting some kind of encouragement, don't contact them a total of more than three or four times (aside from your regular newsletter or update mailings). They'll get annoyed and you'll be wasting time you could be spending on more responsive prospects.

3. Post-show promotion

Many trade show veterans wait to give their strongest leads a giveaway until after the show. Sending them a higher-end gift (a fancy pen, a cool new gadget) two or three days after they get home from the show will set you apart from the crowd. And they'll likely be happy to talk to you when you call to follow up and make sure they received it.

Other ways to promote yourself after the show:

- **Update your company website.** As soon as the show is over, add a page to your site summarizing the show and the products and services featured in your booth. Include photos and links to any trade press articles about your company. Put a link to the show page in any post-show follow-up correspondence you send out.
- **Contact the people you *didn't* meet.** Get a list of attendees from show management (this is free to exhibitors after the show in some cases). Then send a "Sorry we missed you!" email to anyone whose name isn't in your lead data. If you offered any special deals at the show, consider extending them to these contacts. Do this within a week or two after the show while the event is still fresh in attendees' minds.
- **Send out a general mailing.** The next time you send out an update or newsletter, don't forget to mention the show and how successful it was. Some people on your list may have intended to go to the show and not made it. Hearing about it after the fact may prompt them to get in touch with you about new products or even to register next year.

Post-Show Plan

Use this worksheet to plan your post-show follow-up strategy.

How will you organize your lead/contact data?

What method will you use to make your first post-show contact with new leads and contacts?

What will you say? (In an email? A phone call? An in-person meeting?)

When will you schedule your second post-show contact?

What will you say?

What other methods will you use to promote your company/products/show participation after the event?

STEP 1: Choose the Right Show

STEP 2: Book the Show

STEP 3: Create Promotion and Marketing Materials

STEP 4: Merchandise at Your Booth

STEP 5: Turn Browsers into Buyers

STEP 6: Think Outside the Booth

STEP 7: Follow-Up

STEP 8: Evaluate the Show

STEP 9: The Booth

STEP 10: Show Shipments

Accomplishments

In this step you'll:

☐ 1. Learn how to evaluate the value of each trade show you attend

☐ 2. Get tips on how to critique your booth

☐ 3. Assess your overall trade show goals

Time-Saving Tools

You'll complete this step more quickly if you have the following handy:

☐ The goals you established on your "Trade Show Goals" worksheet in Step 1

☐ The "Pre-Show Promotion Plan" you created in Step 3

Step 8: Evaluate the Show

Exhibiting at a trade show or conference takes time, effort, and money. So how do you know whether your investment paid off? Post-show evaluation is an essential part of the trade show planning process. Taking a critical look at your performance at one show will help you make better decisions the next time around.

The most effective way to evaluate your show experience is to break it down into three categories:

- The show itself and the quality of attendees
- Your booth
- Your goals

Once you've assessed your strengths and weaknesses in all three categories, you can decide what—if anything—to change for next time. Even if you manage to hit a home run at your first show, at some point you'll need to refresh and revitalize your booth, your pitch, and your goals. That's why it's important to develop a critical eye from the start.

QUICK**TIP**

Try, Try, Try Again

Your first visit to a particular show or conference isn't necessarily going to indicate how well you'll do in the future. Exhibitors usually need repeat exposure to have an impact. So even if your first time in the booth isn't everything you'd hoped for, if you're sure you're at the right show for your business, give it another try next year.

QUICK**TIP**

The Right Crowd

If none of the attendees you meet at a particular show are a good fit for your business, you'll know not to go back next year. It often takes a bit of trial and error to find the perfect show. The more research you do beforehand (see Step 1 for more details on researching trade shows), the better your odds will be.

1. Critique the show

A show or conference that sounds perfect on paper won't necessarily be the right match for your product or service. Take a critical look at the attendees you met in the booth. Did they fit your criteria for potential customers? If not, why not? If yes, did you have the opportunity to talk to as many of them as you wanted to? Why or why not? What could you or show management have done differently to improve your experience as an exhibitor? Asking questions like these is the best way to evaluate each show you attend.

Use the worksheet below to assess each show's relevance to your company.

Trade Show Evaluation

Name of Show: ______________________________

1. What were your goals for this show? Did you meet them?

____

____

2. How many show attendees did you talk to?

____

3. Why did they come to your booth?

____

____

4. How many of them were qualified leads?

____

5. What was the overall quality of the attendees? How many of them were decision makers or decision influencers?

____

____

6. Would you like to have talked to more people? Fewer?

7. What did you learn about your market as a result of being at the show?

8. Did you implement a Pre-Show Promotion Plan (see Step 3) to drive traffic to your booth? If yes, did it work?

9. What would you change about your Pre-Show Promotion Plan next time?

10. Which networking and social events did you attend? Were they useful?

11. Did you make appointments with existing customers and contacts before the show? If yes, were they productive?

12. Did show management help direct attendees to your booth? How could you work with management better in the future?

13. Overall, how do you *feel* about the show? Do you think it went well? Why or why not?

14. Would you attend this show again in the future? Why or why not?

QUICK**TIP**

A Critical Eye

If you don't get the response you'd hoped for at a show, consider hiring a consultant to observe your booth in action at the next event you attend. Getting an expert's objective opinion of your booth's appearance and staffing can be an eye opener. And if the expert *doesn't* find fault with your booth or your performance, that could be a strong signal that the show wasn't the right fit for you.

2. Critique your booth

Your booth is your home base at every trade show and conference you attend. That makes it an integral part of your show experience. After each event, evaluate whether or not the booth—and how you used it—helped you meet your goals.

Use the worksheet below to assess your booth.

Booth Evaluation

1. Was your booth easy to set up and dismantle? If not, how could it be improved?

2. What were the advantages and disadvantages of your exhibit space location? Where would you like to be next time?

3. Did your booth design and graphics stand out from those of your competitors/other exhibitors? If not, how could you change them?

4. Did you have enough room to display your products and marketing materials? If not, what could you add to your booth next time (or what could you leave behind to make more room)?

5. How well did you staff the booth? Did you have too many people? Too few? How many would you take next time?

6. Did you use technology in your booth? Was it useful/helpful? Would you use it again?

7. Did you offer attendees promotional giveaways? How were they received? Did you give them to only the right people?

8. Were you able to tell quickly whether someone was a qualified lead? If not, how could you refine your questions next time?

9. Was your booth welcoming to attendees? Did anything block the entrance?

10. Was the staff welcoming to attendees? Did booth staffers engage passersby in conversation?

11. How did attendees find your booth? Did they happen upon it or know to come by because of your Pre-Show Promotion Plan? What could you have done to increase the number of visitors?

12. Did you get the right show services in your booth? What would you add/skip next time?

13. Did you take enough of the right supplies? What would you add/skip next time?

3. Assess whether you've met your goals

The clearer your goals are going into a show, the easier it will be to evaluate them after the event. For most exhibitors, the number one goal is to generate leads, which, in turn, bring in sales and new business. Other common show goals:

- Meeting other people in the industry
- Reinforcing existing relationships
- Launching a new product or marketing message
- Raising company visibility
- Seeing what the competition is up to
- Learning more about the industry

It's often difficult to know how to judge or quantify the success of a trade show. You may feel as if you've failed when you come home with only 10 qualified leads. But this is when quality matters much more than quantity. Even *one* order, if it's the right one, can justify your entire trade show investment. One new customer who brings long-term business to your company is worth much more than 100 names to add to your mailing list.

"Softer" show goals, such as maintaining relationships with your existing customers or raising awareness of your company or brand, can be particularly challenging to quantify. While you may not be able to estimate how much extra business comes from taking a client out to dinner, you *can* aim to make appointments with 10 existing customers during the show.

Use the worksheet below to assess whether you've met your goals.

Goal Assessment

1. What was your primary goal going into the show?

____

____

____

2. What were your secondary goals for the show?

____

____

____

3. If your goal was to generate new leads, what was your target number? Did you meet it?

____

____

4. If your goal was to take orders, what was your target number? Did you meet it?

5. Were your goals realistic? If not, how can you refine your goals to be more realistic for your next show?

6. How can you measure your less quantifiable goals?

7. How much new business do you anticipate gaining as a direct result of the show?

8. Did you connect with current and former customers?

9. Did people seem interested in your product or service?

10. Did you get any useful customer feedback about your products or services?

11. Did you make important industry contacts that could lead to new opportunities or strategic partnerships?

12. Did you increase industry exposure to your company/brand?

13. Did you gather important information about your competition? About new developments in your industry?

QUICKTIP

Evaluate Your Pitch

One of the most valuable things you can get out of a trade show is an understanding of which selling points resonate best with your prospects. At the show you can see their faces and you can remember what they ask you and how they respond to your product. This can help you improve your marketing materials and sales pitch in non-trade-show settings as well.

4. Decide what to change for next time

Now that you've taken a closer look at the show, your booth, and your goals, you can decide what you want to do differently at the next event you attend. Use the worksheet below to note changes you'd like to make for future shows.

Future Changes

1. What changes, if any, will you make to your show criteria/selection process?

2. What changes, if any, will you make to your Pre-Show Promotion Plan?

3. What changes, if any, will you make to your booth's appearance?

4. What changes, if any, will you make to your booth staffing?

5. What changes, if any, will you make to your booth location and services?

6. What changes, if any, will you make to your lead-qualification process?

7. What changes, if any, will you make to the way you collect and organize leads?

8. What changes, if any, will you make to your goals?

9. What changes, if any, will you make to your sales pitch?

10. What changes, if any, will you make to your product or service?

11. What changes, if any, will you make to the way you connect with existing customers and contacts?

Revitalize Your Show Experience

It's possible to get stuck in a rut as an exhibitor. Your booth, your sales pitch, and your products may be getting the job done—but could they be getting the job done *better*? Revitalizing your exhibit and your attitude helps you maximize your trade show investment.

- **Try a new show.** Every few years it's important to re-evaluate the shows you attend and see if there are any you should drop or add. If you can afford it, choose a show outside the obvious list and give it a try. At worst, you'll come away with a confirmed sense of the events that are right for you.
- **Ramp up your pre-show promotion.** A well-executed Pre-Show Promotion Plan (see Step 3) is one of the best ways to ensure your show is successful. If you're not already doing pre-show promotion, start. If you are, try something new. Instead of a postcard, try sending an email with a link to all details about when and where you'll be exhibiting. Give those who visit the link the option to pre-register for a booth visit in return for a giveaway item.
- **Try a new at-show promotion.** If you've been giving out logo pens for years, it's time to try something fresh. Use the tips in Step 4 to choose a more creative giveaway. If your budget allows for it, consider doing something splashy during the show: in-booth entertainment, a cocktail party, or a sponsorship.
- **Update your message.** Haven't changed your marketing message in a while? What's new and/or exciting about what you're selling? When you come up with a new message, you can update your exhibit and promotions to match.
- **Update your materials.** Take a fresh look at your marketing materials. Do they showcase your latest products and features? Could they use a re-design? Could they be reformatted to be smaller/more practical/cheaper to print?
- **Update your booth.** Booths are expensive, so it's tempting to keep using them as-is for as long as possible. But rapidly changing trade show trends and innovations mean that booths can end up looking outdated sooner than you'd like. Begin by updating your signs and graphics. This is a much less expensive way to give your booth a new look than buying or renting a whole new booth.
- **Swap out your staff.** If plenty of attendees are coming to your booth but you're not getting the kind of new business you'd like, take a look at who's staffing your exhibit. Small companies often don't have much choice about which staff to send, but if you *do* have options, make sure your staff is committed and excited to be there.
- **Take a field trip.** Need fresh ideas? Go to other industries' shows and see what they're doing. Something that's old hat at a software show might be the height of innovation in the food industry.

STEP 1: Choose the Right Show

STEP 2: Book the Show

STEP 3: Create Promotion and Marketing Materials

STEP 4: Merchandise at Your Booth

STEP 5: Turn Browsers into Buyers

STEP 6: Think Outside the Booth

STEP 7: Follow-Up

STEP 8: Evaluate the Show

STEP 9: The Booth

STEP 10: Show Shipments

Accomplishments

In this step you'll:

☐ 1. Learn about the different types of trade show booths available

☐ 2. Find out where to get a trade show booth

☐ 3. Discover the pros and cons of buying new, buying used, and renting a booth

☐ 4. Get tips and guidelines for effective booth design

☐ 5. Learn how to set up your booth at the show

Time-Saving Tools

You'll complete this step more quickly if you have the following handy:

☐ A list of the shows and conferences you're considering attending (See "Potential Shows" worksheet and "Top Show Choices" worksheet in Step 1)

☐ Your tentative show budget (See "Your Trade Show Budget" worksheet in Step 2)

☐ Your show goals (See "Your Trade Show Goals" worksheet in Step 1)

☐ Information on your target customer (See "Target Customer Profile," "Potential Target Customers," and "Most Wanted List" worksheets in Step 1)

Step 9: The Booth

Your booth is whatever you use to display your products and services in your exhibit space. A trade show booth is designed to provide exhibitors with a:

- Presence and home base at the show
- Way to attract and qualify new leads
- Place to meet with attendees
- Place to display and demonstrate a product or service (and possibly to sell it)
- Showcase for establishing company or brand identity
- Good impression for attendees to remember when they return home

> QUICK**TIP**
>
> **Third Time's a Charm**
>
> **Once you're regularly attending three or more trade shows or conferences per year, it's time to buy a booth. Until you hit that magic number, renting might make more economic sense, but after that, purchasing your own booth becomes a smart investment.**

That's why most exhibitors choose to buy or rent a professionally designed and manufactured booth. Many options are available, from inexpensive portable stands to complex two-story mini-arenas. The key is to work within your budget to find an affordable, professional solution.

Some smaller shows and conferences either discourage or simply don't allow exhibitors to use anything except the flat surface of one or two tables (hence the term "tabletop show"). If that's the kind of event you're attending, you don't need a booth.

1. Booth types

Once you've attended a few trade shows and conferences, you'll realize that "booth" is a relative term. The soaring, sprawling complexes erected by some large companies are more like architectural achievements. No one expects you to compete with those custom-designed marvels. But it's still good to know that those kinds of displays are out there, since you want to be aware of all your options before making a decision. All the booth types listed below can be purchased through an exhibit display company. When you choose a company, its employees will work with you on design, graphics, and all the other necessary details.

When You *Don't* Need a Booth

At some smaller, more casual trade shows and conferences, professionally designed booths are not the norm. If you show up at these events with crates full of graphics and lighting, you'll stick out like a sore thumb. At these events—often called "tabletop shows"—exhibitors must restrict their display to what will fit on top of one or two tables. Other events where you probably won't need a booth:

- Small local events like Chamber of Commerce mixers
- Meetings of regional branches of industry associations
- Client seminars and open houses
- Hospitality events

The most common types of exhibit booths:

	REALISTIC FOR NEW EXHIBITORS?	WHAT IT LOOKS LIKE	HOW IT WORKS	TYPICAL COST
Pop-Up	Yes. This type of booth is the most commonly used. Pop-ups are typical for small exhibitors in 10' x 10' spaces.	Usually curved like a wide "C" and 6'–8' tall by 6'–10' wide. Typically constructed with lightweight metal frames and vinyl panels (fabric panels may also be an option) that are printed with custom/branded graphics.	Designed to be assembled and disassembled easily and fit inside special storage cases that can double as tables/stands. Metal frames collapse for storage and "pop up" for assembly.	$800–$4,000
Tabletop*	Yes. A smaller version of the pop-up. Most are designed to sit on top of a standard 6' table for shows that don't allow booths.	Just like a pop-up, but smaller—usually 3'–6' tall by 4'–8' wide. Tabletops' frame-and-panel construction is just like that of a pop-up.	Like pop-ups, designed to be assembled and disassembled easily and to fit inside a portable storage case.	$250–$1,800

* As a booth type, "tabletop" refers to a small, pop-up exhibit that sits on top of a table. This differs from the definition of a tabletop *show*, which restricts exhibitors to using the actual table surface itself—without any kind of exhibit on top.

	REALISTIC FOR NEW EXHIBITORS?	WHAT IT LOOKS LIKE	HOW IT WORKS	TYPICAL COST
Modular	No, unless you have a large trade show budget and you're planning on renting a space larger than 10' x 10'.	A center display forms the core of a larger exhibit that operates on the frame-and-panel principles but spreads out in different directions with multiple stations for booth staffers and visitors.	Most involve some variation on the frame-and-panel assembly, but some designs also incorporate fabric, shelving, and workstations. Designed for relatively easy assembly, disassembly, and storage.	$2,000–$15,000
Custom	No. Custom booths are designed for big companies with huge budgets who will be renting large anchor positions on the show floor.	The only limits are imagination and budget. Often built around a core "island," with outlying stations. Can be multi-story, with conference rooms and theaters.	Custom displays are complex and usually require several days' work by multiple people to install and dismantle.	Start at $20,000 and go up.

QUICK**TIP**

On the Cheap

You don't have to have a booth at all. Most trade shows offer a basic exhibit registration package that includes a draped table and a chair or two. If you're new to trade shows, this is an inexpensive way to get started. Combine a table with a banner (see page 145) for more impact.

2. Where to get a booth

The easiest way to get a new trade show booth decorated with your company logo and graphics is to find an exhibit display company and work with them to produce an exhibit. To find the right firm, use resources like:

- **The phone book.** Check your local yellow pages for exhibit companies in your area. Look under "Display Designers," "Exhibit Builders," "Trade Shows," "Expositions," and "Convention Services."
- **The Internet.** Use a search engine to query the terms listed above, paired with the name of your city/area. Many national companies have branches throughout the country.
- **Word of mouth.** Ask your friends, customers, and partners for recommendations. And when you attend trade shows, look for exhibits you like and ask who made them.

Once you've assembled a list of exhibit display companies in your area, contact them for product information and price quotes. It will help if you have a good idea of what you want to buy before you call. For most small businesses, a tabletop or pop-up exhibit is the most realistic place to start. In order to give you an accurate estimate, the companies on your list may want to see some of your current marketing materials (to get a sense of your brand and style) and find out:

- Where you're planning to exhibit
- What products or services you'd like to display in your booth
- Who your target customers are
- What your goals are for the shows you plan to attend
- How much you have to spend
- When the display needs to be completed

Be sure to do your own research too. Ask the companies on your list if you can speak with former or current clients. Find out what kinds of experiences these people had working with the company. Were the consultants and designers easy to work with? Did the work get done well, on time, and on budget? Would they work with the company again?

After you choose a display company, you'll likely have several meetings to decide on a style and design for your exhibit. Be honest with the designers. Tell them what you want and what your budget is. But listen to their suggestions too—after all, they design exhibits for a living. Use the following worksheets to keep track of exhibit display companies from which you've requested estimates.

Company Name:

____

Address: ____________________

Phone number: ____________________

Email: ____________________

Website URL (if applicable): ____________________

Date information/price quote requested: ____________________

Date information/price quote received: ____________________

Notes: ____________________

Company Name:

Address:

Phone number:

Email:

Website URL (if applicable):

Date information/price quote requested:

Date information/price quote received:

Notes:

Company Name:

Address:

Phone number:

Email:

Website URL (if applicable):

Date information/price quote requested:

Date information/price quote received:

Notes:

Exhibit Display Information

Fill out this worksheet and give a copy to all the exhibit display companies you're considering.

Where I'm exhibiting:

What I'll be displaying in the booth:

My target customers:

My show goals:

My booth budget:

My booth deadline:

3. Alternatives to buying new

When you're ready to invest in a trade show booth, buying a brand-new exhibit isn't your only option. Many businesses rent booths if they're attending only one or two shows a year or want to make a bigger splash at a particular show than their usual display would make. Some companies save money by purchasing used booths and updating them with their own logo and graphics.

	PROS	CONS
Renting	• If you're exhibiting at fewer than three shows per year, renting can be more cost effective than buying a new booth (rentals are often less than $1,000 per show). • Most rental fees include shipping and storage costs. • No need to store a bulky booth. • If you don't like the type of exhibit you rent, you can try another type next time. • If you already own a small exhibit, you can rent expansion parts for specific shows.	• The booth quality may not be as high as you'd like. • You need to supply your own graphics, which may not work perfectly with the booth you rent and will be an additional expense. • You likely won't be able to inspect the exhibit until you arrive at the show. • If you rent different types of exhibits at different shows, you will need to buy multiple graphics options, and this can get expensive. • The cost of frequent renting can add up.
Buying	• Your booth is designed specifically for you, with your graphics and goals in mind. • You know exactly what you're working with before the show, which can make planning easier. • Familiarity with your exhibit means you can focus on attendees.	• You're responsible for storage and shipping. • You may realize after purchasing your booth that it doesn't meet your needs. • Buying a booth is a significant expense. • You have the same booth, year after year.

	PROS	CONS
Used	• Less expensive than buying a new booth. • Smaller investment makes it easier/more realistic for new exhibitors to test the trade show waters.	• Many are still expensive, often more than half the cost of a new booth. • You'll need to refurbish it and update it with your own company graphics, creating an additional expense. • As with any used purchase, you never know exactly what you're going to get.
New	• Your booth is designed specifically for you, with your graphics and goals in mind. • You know exactly what to expect from your exhibit, since you're involved in every step of its design and creation.	• Buying a brand-new booth is expensive. • You may realize after purchasing your booth that it doesn't meet your needs.

If you decide to buy a used exhibit, check the sources listed on page 139. Most exhibit display companies also sell used booths. Also check websites like eBay.com and ExhibitAuction.com for good deals.

If you opt to rent, ask the show services department at the show(s) you're planning to attend if they offer rentals. Check with exhibit display companies in your area or in the location of the trade show to find out if they rent booths.

In the end, the best booth option for your company depends on your budget, the number of shows you plan to attend, show goals, and other factors such as the corporate image you want to present. But if you want a strong presence on the show floor and you've decided to exhibit regularly at trade shows and conferences, buy the best booth you can afford. Having your own professionally designed booth is the best way to convey the right message to attendees, which, in turn, helps you convert them into qualified leads.

A Banner Event

Professionally designed booths are not your only choice for making a splash in the exhibition hall, especially at smaller shows. Two creative alternatives to combine with a draped table (usually included in your trade show registration):

- **Banner stands.** Many exhibit companies sell these inexpensive displays, which consist of a vinyl or fabric panel that retracts into a portable tube/stand. When customized with your graphics, banner stands are a practical, professional-looking option, especially for new exhibitors. They are typically about 7′ tall and 3′–4′ wide and cost only a few hundred dollars.
- **Banners.** For a few hundred dollars, you can create a vinyl banner featuring your company name, logo, and slogan to hang in or above your exhibit space. Companies that specialize in digital printing, as well as those that print postcards and brochures, can create these for you if you supply the digital files. Be sure to check with show management about rules for hanging banners. Not all venues permit tacks or nails in their walls. If this is the case, consider adding Velcro to the back of your banner or metal rivets along the top so you can hang it with cord.

QUICK**TIP**

Curtain Up!

Many trade show pros compare designing and setting up a booth to putting on a play, and for good reason. Think of your booth as a stage. Everything inside it should help your actors (booth staffers) put on a convincing performance (accomplish your show goals). Your graphics become your props and eye-catching backdrops, your lighting is designed to flatter and illuminate, and if your production is a success, instead of a standing ovation, you get new business!

4. What should your booth look like?

The decision to buy a booth is only the first of many booth-related choices you'll have to make. You also have to decide what it will look like and what you want to include inside it. If you're working with an exhibit display company, they can provide helpful advice and input based on your goals and their own experience.

Keep in mind when you're considering what to include in your booth:

- **If your goal is to promote a product (or products),** you need to display samples of the product(s) you want to promote. Look for ways to help showcase your products: built-in shelves, racks to put on top of a stand or table, and so on. If your company has many products, focus on the ones that will provide the biggest benefit to your target customers. (These may or may not be your newest offerings.) Having too many products in your booth can be cluttered and confusing, so streamline.
- **If your goal is to promote a service,** you need a way to communicate its benefits as well as your company's accomplishments. You can use graphics for the former, and for the latter, consider portfolios or binders that showcase successfully completed jobs. Be sure to highlight any notable clients.
- **If your goal is to promote your company's identity,** it all comes down to your graphics, which are the key component of your booth display. When your main goal is to promote your identity, it's more important than ever to make sure your graphics clearly convey the information attendees are looking for.

QUICKTIP

Places, Everyone

The best position for key graphics is at the top of your display. People tend to read from top to bottom. So the higher the placement of your logo, company name, and tagline, the more visible they'll be from the aisle. And putting important graphics up high reduces the risk of staffers blocking them so attendees can't see them.

Booth Graphics 101

Graphics are by far the most important component of your booth. With so many exhibitors competing for attendees' attention and time, your graphics need to help you stand out from the crowd. (Graphics include your logo, colors, type styles, taglines, and other design elements that help to identify your company.)

You won't have to start from scratch when it's time to design your booth graphics. Your trade show booth is part of your overall marketing campaign. So you can re-purpose the logos and other design elements you already use in brochures, advertisements, and other marketing materials. Keeping your graphics consistent throughout your different marketing vehicles saves time and helps cement your identity and your message.

But be aware that one of the fastest ways to end up with an unimpressive-looking booth is to simply enlarge a picture from your corporate website and use it as-is in your booth graphics. Think of your existing design elements as an *inspiration* or *starting point,* but make sure your booth graphics are crafted to work within an exhibit space. A graphic that works on a website or brochure may not translate well into a booth display. If you're working with an exhibit display company to design your booth, their designers will help you with this.

Your graphics need to do more than look good. They also need to communicate three key pieces of information:

- Who you are
- What you do
- Why/how you do it better than your competitors

QUICK**TIP**

Making the Most of Your Booth

Your booth doesn't have to be consigned to storage between shows. If you have space in your office reception area, consider assembling all or part of the booth for display there. Presto: You've got an attention-grabbing, branded display out where lots of people will see it. Of course, having the booth in a high-traffic area can increase the likelihood of wear and tear, so make sure it's secure and well protected.

Using your logo in your graphics (along with your company name if the logo doesn't make it clear) is the fastest way to communicate who you are. But unless you're General Motors, Apple, or eBay, your graphics also need to tell people what you do. This can be conveyed through pictures—of your products (if they're photogenic enough) or of symbols that represent your products (computers and CDs if you sell software, for example)—or through text. But note that it's best to keep words to a minimum. If you illustrate with pictures, choose images that are easy to comprehend from a distance. You want attendees to be able to understand what you do from the aisle.

You also need to communicate to your target audience what sets you apart from your competitors—the benefits you offer. Use a tagline that conveys both what you do and what separates you from the crowd.

Like everything involving the booth, your graphics should be designed with your show goals in mind:

- If your goal is to generate leads, your graphics should emphasize the benefits of your product, service, or company.
- If your goal is to launch a new product, your graphics should focus on that particular product and its benefits.
- If your goal is to create awareness of who you are as a company, your graphics should emphasize your logo and your reputation in the industry.

If you have different goals at different shows, you'll have to create different graphics that you can swap in and out as necessary. Most booths are designed with that possibility in mind.

Tips on Colors and Text

Consider these guidelines on colors and text when designing your booth graphics:

- **Color.** Make sure colors are consistent with your existing corporate branding. If your logo is red and yellow, it doesn't make sense to design your booth graphics in shades of blue and green.
- **Text size.** A good rule of thumb is to make sure that none of the lettering on your graphics is less than 2 inches high. Headlines—featuring the name of your company, specific products, or key benefits—should be larger. Attendees will be trying to read your graphics from 10' to 12' away in the middle of the aisle. Make it easy for them.
- **Text length.** Limit all important phrases (including your tagline) to 7 words or less. Think of your graphics as a billboard. Simple, legible copy is key.
- **Supporting text.** If you decide to include smaller, benefit-oriented text in your graphics (bullet points listing your product's features, for example), position it in the lower portion of the exhibit. This text will be more useful to booth staffers than to attendees: When you're talking to prospects, you can use the information printed on the graphics as conversation prompts.

Color Significance

Certain colors have specific associations. You may want to keep these in mind as you choose the colors for your booth graphics:

- **Red:** power, energy, danger; associated with good luck in the Asian community
- **Green:** growth, movement, healing; associated with the environmental movement
- **Blue:** stability, calm, security, business; associated with water-related images
- **Yellow:** cheerful, uplifting
- **Purple:** associated with spiritual meanings for some people
- **White:** purity, honesty; associated with spirituality by some communities and with mourning by others

Booth Lighting

Lighting plays an important part in your booth's overall look and feel. Use lights to:

- **Stand out from the crowd.** If your booth is brighter than your neighbors', it will stand out.
- **Focus attention on a particular part of your display.** Whether it's a graphic or a product, anything that has a spotlight shining on it will catch people's attention.
- **Introduce motion into your display.** Flashing or moving lights will draw attendees' eyes. But they might also annoy your neighbors or be against show rules, so check with show management before setting up anything that smacks of Las Vegas.

Most professionally designed booths come complete with some strategically placed lighting, but if you want to add more or if you're exhibiting without a booth, don't hesitate to take your own lighting to the show. If you have electricity in your exhibit space, inexpensive clip lights can be attached to the dividers between booths. They can then be positioned to shine on whatever you want to highlight. A small lamp can be placed on top of a table to add warmth and illuminate a portfolio of past projects.

Technology in the Booth

Laptop computers, big-screen TVs, DVD players, and other technology have become an integral part of many trade show booths.

Computers are most often used for:

- In-booth product demonstrations and presentations (displayed on large, easy-to-see TVs or monitors)
- Capturing and organizing lead information during the show

DVD players can be used for:

- Playing pre-recorded demos
- Playing a highlight reel of past projects and client endorsements

If you have a good reason to use technology in your booth, do it. But technology for technology's sake can become a distraction. If having a computer in your booth gets in the way of making a personal connection with potential leads, it's not worth it.

When you're deciding what technology, if any, to include in your booth, consider these factors:

- If attendees see a computer in your booth, they may flock to you ... so they can check sports scores or email. Be prepared for the challenge of distinguishing true potential leads from Web junkies.

- Use up-to-date equipment, especially if it's on public display. Like it or not, everyone judges by appearances.
- Don't leave expensive machinery unattended in your booth. If you have to leave the booth, either take your computer with you or ask a trusted neighbor to watch over it. Some shows offer technology rentals, which may be a good option if you're worried about theft.
- Shipping large monitors and TVs can be very expensive. Consider a rental or buy one cheaply from a local retailer and make it the grand prize in a giveaway at the end of the show.
- If you rent any equipment, check to make sure it will work with the rest of your system. Take any necessary cables or connectors with you, and find out ahead of time where the nearest electronics store is in case of emergency. Always take instruction manuals.

Keep It Clean

When you have your laptop computer hooked up to a big-screen TV for demos and presentations, the last thing you want is to have the computer fall asleep and display a screen-saver photo of your dog.

The best way to avoid any computer-related snafus at trade shows and conferences is to take a machine dedicated to demos and presentations. If that's not an option, be sure to do the following before using your personal computer in the booth:

- Turn off all sounds and audio alerts.
- Replace any personal desktop background or screen-saver photos with a generic background. Better yet, use your logo.
- Turn off your computer's automatic sleep settings so it won't flip to a screen saver every 15 minutes.
- Remove all sensitive documents from the computer.
- If you have Internet access in the booth, make sure all instant messenger applications are disabled.

QUICK**TIP**

Clothing Counts

If you set up your booth the day before the trade show, wear something comfortable and flexible but not sloppy. Show management and other exhibitors will be passing through the exhibition hall, and your appearance during set-up and take down will make an impression.

5. Set up your booth

When your booth arrives, don't just put it away until it's time to go to the trade show. Practice setting it up and taking it down. Most exhibit display firms will include assembly and breakdown training as part of your package. But it's one thing to follow a pro's instructions and quite another to wrangle the metal frames and vinyl panels by yourself.

Practice until you can set up the booth easily. Take notes and photos, and take them with you to the show. When those poles won't fit back into the container, having a photo of how you did it before could make a big difference. Time your set-up so you know how long you'll need to put your booth together on the exhibition floor. Put up your graphics and place your products on the tables and shelves to see how your booth will look to attendees. If it's too crowded, remove low-priority items. If it looks too bare, add multiples of anything you want to promote. Take note of exactly how many of each item you'll need for the booth and add this to your packing list. Practice attaching your graphics to the booth and be sure to add these materials to your list as well. When you're satisfied with the way your booth looks, take a photo so you can duplicate the arrangement when you're at the show.

If you've practiced unpacking and assembling and disassembling and repacking, you'll feel comfortable doing everything yourself when you arrive at the show. Check your registration materials to see when you are allowed to enter the exhibition hall, and arrive in time to set up the booth before the show floor opens.

With pictures, practice, and a plan, you should have little trouble setting up your booth.

STEP 1: Choose the Right Show

STEP 2: Book the Show

STEP 3: Create Promotion and Marketing Materials

STEP 4: Merchandise at Your Booth

STEP 5: Turn Browsers into Buyers

STEP 6: Think Outside the Booth

STEP 7: Follow-Up

STEP 8: Evaluate the Show

STEP 9: The Booth

STEP 10: Show Shipments

Accomplishments

In this step you'll:

☐ 1. Find out what, how, and when to ship to the show

☐ 2. Learn how to get it all home again safely

Time-Saving Tools

You'll complete this step more quickly if you have the following handy:

☐ Exhibitor materials (if you've already registered for a show)

☐ Your calendar (to note deadlines, including shipping dates)

Step 10: Show Shipments

Booking floor space, sending in exhibit paperwork, and making travel arrangements aren't the only logistics-related items on your trade show checklist. You still need to get all of your material and equipment, from your booth to your business cards, to the exhibition hall and then get it home again when the show is over.

Preparing your show shipments doesn't have to be painful. If you begin planning six weeks before the show, you'll have plenty of time to get everything—products, marketing materials, exhibit graphics—where it needs to go without panicking or paying for express shipping fees.

You'll find that some smaller shows prohibit shipments from arriving more than a few days before the show begins. As always with trade shows and conferences, the trick is to know the rules and regulations.

QUICK**TIP**

Spare Me!

For most shows, you will ship promotional materials such as brochures, sales sheets, and catalogs ahead of time. But be sure to take a spare set with you, in case anything gets lost and you need to make more copies or reprint at the last minute. Take both electronic and hard copies, and keep them in your carry-on luggage, rather than in checked bags.

1. Shipping to the show

After you reserve your exhibit space, you should receive an exhibitor manual (or packet or binder) from show management. The shipping section of the manual will likely include information about both freight and drayage costs (see below), as well as the names of recommended carriers.

It's important to know how show logistics work at all levels. Be familiar with these terms:

- **Freight shipping (sometimes called "shipping").** This is the shipment method to use when you're sending at least 200 pounds of items to the show. Materials are stacked on pallets, shrink-wrapped, and then sent by truck to the show location. Minimum weight requirements usually apply, and round-trip shipping is assumed. The advantages of using a show's recommended carrier include possible discounts and the assurance that you're working with a company familiar with the show and venue. Most recommended carriers listed in show manuals are for ground freight shipping only. If you're not shipping by ground, other options include air freight services, van lines, and, for smaller quantities, a package-shipping company like UPS, FedEx, or USPS.
- **Drayage.** Drayage is the fee that exhibitors are charged to have their materials moved from the show's receiving dock to their exhibit space on the show floor. Sending your equipment to the show venue doesn't mean it actually gets all the way to your exhibit location. You have to pay more for that. Even smaller shows will charge a few dollars per box to transport materials from the "holding" area to the exhibit location on the show floor.
- **Common carrier.** A common carrier is a type of ground freight transportation service that groups small shipments together into big ones. Using a common carrier can be less expensive than other shipping methods, but it often takes a lot longer. And since shipments are continually being consolidated, your items will probably be moved around and handled more often than if they're sent another way.

What to Ship

Many trade show exhibitors think they can take everything they need with them on the plane. Saving the money you'd use to ship exhibit materials separately is tempting, but it's not practical to turn yourself into a human pack horse. You'll be exhausted before the show begins, and if bags are large or heavy, you may end up paying extra to get them on the plane.

Ship the following to the show ahead of time:

- **Booth/exhibit.** Even the smallest pop-up booths are generally stored in protective, plastic containers. This reduces the risk of damage if you send them ahead of time. And it's much easier to let a shipping company deal with them. Make sure all parts of your booth are in the cases. Using a vinyl backdrop? Roll it up in a poster tube and send it in advance.

- **Products.** As long as your products aren't bulky or heavy, pack 1 or 2 samples in your luggage, just in case. Send the rest along ahead of time, especially if you're shipping a large quantity to sell at the show.

- **Marketing materials.** Keep electronic and hard copies of all key marketing materials with you from the time you leave the office until the show is over. You may need to have some items reprinted on-site. Send all pre-printed copies to the show ahead of time. They'll be too heavy and bulky for you to take with you on the plane.

- **Business cards.** You'll want to take at least a few hundred cards (depending on the size of the show). Send most of them ahead of time, reserving a handful to carry with you.

- **Booth supplies.** Ship anything you might need in the booth: tape, scissors, lights. If you're planning to attend several shows, buy a set of show-dedicated supplies and keep them together in one box. When it's time to get your shipments ready, all you have to do is seal the box and stick on a label.

QUICK**TIP**

Don't Miss Out

Some shows assign exhibitors specific move-in dates. If your materials aren't there at the scheduled time, you'll miss out on having them delivered to your exhibit space. Then you may have to wait until everyone else is set up before your materials make it to your space.

When to Ship

When you ship your exhibit and other materials to the show venue depends on the type of show you're attending.

- **Larger shows** usually take place at big conference centers with shipping and receiving areas. So they will typically accept shipments a few weeks before the event begins. Look at your exhibitor materials to find out the first and last dates that show management will allow shipments to arrive. Take advantage of large shows' long receiving window, and send your materials ahead of time. If you ship early, you'll have more time to confirm that your boxes have arrived safely before you get on the plane.

- **Smaller shows** usually take place at hotels. This means they don't have unlimited space to store exhibit materials, and they often won't accept shipments until a day or two before the event begins. If you have your boxes ready to go, you can ship your packages by ground a week before the receiving window opens, and everything will still get there on time. But small shows will sometimes enforce a "don't ship before" date. If you send things ahead of that day, show management may charge you a penalty fee.

It's possible to ship your marketing materials at the last minute using overnight express service. But that's expensive and impractical. Study your exhibitor materials carefully as soon as they arrive, and note all shipping-relevant dates on your calendar. Then stick to them. If you have questions, don't hesitate to call show management.

QUICK**TIP**

Number, Please

If you know your booth number ahead of time, put it on *everything* you send to the show. Write the number on every side of all your boxes so it can't be missed. Be sure to put "Booth #" in front of the digits. On its own, the number can easily get lost amidst the other information on your packages.

Where to Ship

The best place to ship your show materials is wherever show management tells you to send them. Typically, when you register as an exhibitor, your show materials will include shipping labels (or at least a sample) that you can use when preparing your boxes and other shipments. These labels usually include the following information:

- Venue name and address
- Name of show/conference
- Show/conference dates

Larger shows at convention centers will always have a specific shipping address, no matter what carrier exhibitors are using. (The possible exception is for exhibitors sending pallets of materials that need to be moved with a forklift. Some shows have a separate address for these extra-large arrivals.) Smaller shows at hotels usually ask exhibitors to address shipments to the attention of the on-site conference manager, so be sure to include that information on all your labels.

Call ahead to see if your boxes have arrived before you leave for the show. If you're sending things to a hotel, the front desk might not have that information. Ask to speak to the conference coordinator instead. Typically, show-related shipments will be held in receiving (conference centers) or in a designated storage area/room (hotels) until the exhibition area is ready for set-up. Then everything will be delivered to your booth. It's that delivery that triggers drayage or other transportation fees.

There's no reason to send things to any location other than the address specified by show management. (There is only one possible exception: if you have no choice but to ship outside the date range specified by management.) If you ship your boxes to another hotel or to friends or family in the area, you'll still have to figure out how to transport everything to the exhibition hall.

Choosing a Shipping Company

As long as you're not shipping hundreds of pounds' worth of gear and equipment to the show, you don't need to use the show's recommended carrier(s). Exhibitors who have only a few boxes to ship can use a package-shipping company such as UPS, FedEx, or DHL or the U.S. Postal Service. Just make sure that the service you choose meets these criteria:

- **Shipments are trackable.** At any given moment, you should be able to find out exactly where your boxes are. You should also be able to verify their safe arrival.
- **Competitive price.** Most shipping companies can provide rate estimates online. Pack a sample box, weigh and measure it, then shop around for the best price.
- **Reliable.** Money isn't everything. If a shipping company doesn't have a reputation for reliable service, don't entrust your exhibit, products, or marketing materials to their care.

Preparing Your Shipments

For the most part, getting your trade show materials ready for shipping is just like preparing any other business package: pack carefully and use a trusted carrier that provides tracking numbers.

Other guidelines:

- **Use strong, high-quality boxes.** You'll be using the same boxes to ship things home from the show.
- **Consolidate.** The fewer boxes you send, the fewer you have to keep track of. Don't overload boxes or send huge packages filled to the brim with heavy materials. But try to avoid sending more individual items than absolutely necessary.
- **Number your boxes.** On each package, note that it's "1 of 6" (or whichever number it is). When you get to your exhibit space, you'll be able to tell at a glance if everything's there.
- **Try a stress test.** Be sure your boxes can take a little abuse. Pack up a test box, including some "dummy" items you are not concerned about breaking. Then hold it straight out in front of you at arm's length and drop it. If the box and the breakables are intact, your package can handle stress.
- **Insure it.** Insure your trade show shipments for whatever value you place on having your materials there on time and in good condition.

QUICK**TIP**

Take Inventory

As you prepare your boxes for shipment, make a list of what you've packed in each one and take it with you to the show. That way you'll know which box to open first—ideally, the one with the scissors, tape, and other set-up items!

If you have the time and resources, consider boxing and labeling a set of back-up materials (brochures, catalogs, product samples) to leave at the office. In case of emergency—a shipment gone astray, booth theft—you'll have everything ready for someone to ship to you overnight.

What *Not* to Ship

No matter how reliable your shipping company is, some trade show supplies and materials shouldn't be trusted to anyone. Packages can get lost or delayed. Even if your shipment is on time, you'll probably need documents like your registration and booth paperwork before you have a chance to get to your exhibit space and unpack.

These items should travel with you to the show—not in your shipping boxes:

- **All show-related paperwork.** Keep with you at all times anything that proves you have a right to be at the show and have paid for specific features and services.
- **Extra copies of marketing materials.** Keep electronic and hard copies of all marketing materials with you in case you need to get extras printed up at the last minute.
- **Extra business cards.** Keep a day's worth of spares with you in case your boxes are delayed. You may also need them if you go to a networking event before you make it to the booth.
- **Practical items.** Make sure to carry something that you can use to open boxes. Keys are your best bet, since scissors and box cutters will need to be shipped ahead or sent in checked luggage. It's always a good idea to have a pen and at least one spare handy too.

Checklist: Shipping to the Show

Use this checklist to keep track of everything you'll be taking to the show.

SHIP AHEAD OF TIME:

Booth/exhibit materials

- ☐ Booth
- ☐ Banners and signs
- ☐ Product display holders
- ☐ Lights
- ☐ Photos and illustrations
- ☐ Computers and audiovisual equipment

Products/Product Samples

- ☐ New products
- ☐ Existing products
- ☐ Past projects binder

Marketing Materials

- ☐ Catalogs
- ☐ Order forms
- ☐ Brochures
- ☐ Sales sheets
- ☐ Business cards
- ☐ Giveaways
- ☐ Other:

Booth Supplies

- ☐ Lead forms or trade show notebooks
- ☐ Pens
- ☐ Stapler
- ☐ String
- ☐ Packing tape
- ☐ Permanent marker
- ☐ Shipping labels
- ☐ Shipping envelopes/ materials and paperwork
- ☐ A pad of plain notepaper
- ☐ An appointment book/ calendar for making follow-up appointments
- ☐ Order forms
- ☐ Other:

Other Useful Items

- ☐ Antibacterial hand sanitizer
- ☐ Wet wipes
- ☐ Spray cleaner and paper towels
- ☐ Hand vacuum
- ☐ Duct tape
- ☐ Scissors
- ☐ Universal screwdriver
- ☐ Pliers
- ☐ Box cutter
- ☐ 3-to-2-prong plug converter
- ☐ Extra lightbulbs
- ☐ Batteries
- ☐ Extension cords
- ☐ Power strip
- ☐ Flashlight
- ☐ Plastic bags with zip closures
- ☐ Other:

Personal Items

- ☐ Bottled water
- ☐ Dry snacks
- ☐ Breath mints
- ☐ Small first aid kit

TAKE WITH YOU:

- ☐ Show paperwork
- ☐ Electronic copies of marketing materials
- ☐ Hard copies of marketing materials
- ☐ Extra business cards
- ☐ Extra pen(s)
- ☐ Keys (for opening boxes)
- ☐ A list of emergency contact information
- ☐ Extra lead forms or trade show notebooks

Personal Packing

After the last box of trade show supplies has left your office, it's time to think about what to pack for yourself. Include anything you need to feel comfortable and energized while you're at the show.

- **Comfortable shoes.** Take at least two pairs. Even the most comfortable shoes will pinch and rub after a long day on the show floor. If you can switch to another pair the next day, you'll be more comfortable. Take shoes with different heights of heels if you can.
- **Foot soak and/or lotion.** In addition to comfortable shoes, take something to reinvigorate your tired toes at the end of the day.
- **Comfortable clothes.** When you're in a hotel room, there's no need to dress up.
- **Booth wardrobe.** Take an extra set of clothes, especially if you're using logo wear. You'll get dirty, and accidents happen.
- **Electronic device chargers.** Don't forget to take chargers for your cell phone, BlackBerry, and computer.

2. Shipping from the show

When the last attendee has left the exhibition hall and the last business card has been exchanged, it's time to pack up and ship everything home. Planning ahead will make the process go smoothly.

If you gave away products and marketing materials, you'll likely have less to send home than you had to ship out. But there will still be material left to wrangle.

To get your home-bound packages ready:

- Prepare return shipping labels ahead of time. Take completed or blank labels with you (or get them from show management or the hotel business center) and fill them out well before it's time to leave.
- Stow your exhibit in its custom/special cases. Your booth should always travel in the containers provided for it.
- Pack leftover materials and supplies in the same boxes you used to send them to the show. Pack up any marketing materials you collected from other exhibitors too.
- Check your exhibit space to make sure you haven't left anything behind.
- When you get to the last box, pre-cut some strips of packing tape to seal that box. Then toss the tape dispenser inside and close up the box. That way you won't have to clutter up your carry-on bag with a tape dispenser.
- Fill out your return shipping labels and attach them to your sealed boxes.

QUICK**TIP**

Box It Up

If you store your boxes in your booth during the show, they'll be nearby when it's time to pack up. If you store them with show services, you'll have to wait around after the end of the exhibition until show staffers take them back. And there's always the chance you could be last on the list! So if you have room in your booth, keep your boxes close.

QUICK**TIP**

Order Up!

If you're going to be taking orders at a show, don't forget to take order forms, credit card processing equipment, and anything else you need to complete your sales. A word of caution: Shows that involve taking orders are challenging to do alone. It's difficult to process one person's order and answer questions from another booth visitor at the same time. Consider taking a co-worker with you.

What happens next is up to show management. Read your exhibitor materials carefully to find out the process for sending materials home. If the paperwork doesn't give you the information you need, ask management.

Some shows allow you to leave your packed boxes in your booth, where they'll be picked up and shipped out for you. When show management does *not* offer in-booth pickup service, take your boxes to the front desk (if the show is at a hotel) or to the on-site shipping facilities (if the show is at a large conference center) to have them sent back. Get tracking numbers, if possible.

On-Site Shipping

Shows held at convention centers usually have an on-site shipping booth. The booth may be in the exhibition hall or it may be in the lobby. It should be stocked with supplies and staffed by people who can answer your shipping-related questions.

Anyone at the show—attendees and exhibitors alike—can use on-site shipping facilities to send packages out during and after the show. If you are not having your boxes picked up at your booth, pack them and take them to the shipping booth. Fill out any necessary forms while you're in line. Or if someone else is with you, one of you can wait in line while the other finishes packing up in the booth.

What *Not* to Ship Home

Just as there are certain items you should always carry with you on your way to a trade show or conference, there are some things you shouldn't trust to anyone else on the way back.

Some of your items will be in the "can't-afford-to-lose" category. Keep them with you at all times.

- **Lead data or trade show notebook.** Your lead data is your most valuable show asset, and you need to start using it for follow-up as soon as you get back to the office. Don't risk putting it in a package that could get lost or delayed.
- **Orders.** Just like lead data, completed order forms and receipts are both valuable and time sensitive. If you have products to ship, you need to do that right away.
- **Pressing action items.** Will you have calls to make during the first day or two you're back in the office? Follow-up promises to fulfill? Any notes related to important action items should travel home in your carry-on bags.
- **Shipping forms.** Keep copies of all return-shipping forms with you. You may need the tracking numbers if something goes astray.
- **Show management phone numbers.** If you encounter problems with booth pickup or dismantling after you depart, you'll need to contact someone from show management.

Checklist: Shipping from the Show

Use this checklist to keep track of everything you'll be sending home from the show.

SHIP AHEAD OF TIME:

Booth/exhibit materials

- ☐ Booth
- ☐ Banners and signs
- ☐ Product display holders
- ☐ Lights
- ☐ Photos and illustrations
- ☐ Computers and audiovisual equipment

Products/Product Samples

- ☐ New products
- ☐ Existing products
- ☐ Past projects binder

Marketing Materials

- ☐ Catalogs
- ☐ Order forms
- ☐ Brochures
- ☐ Sales sheets
- ☐ Business cards
- ☐ Giveaways
- ☐ Other:

Booth Supplies

- ☐ Pens
- ☐ Stapler
- ☐ String
- ☐ Packing tape
- ☐ Permanent marker
- ☐ Shipping labels
- ☐ Shipping envelopes/ materials and paperwork
- ☐ A pad of plain notepaper
- ☐ Other:

Other Useful Items

- ☐ Antibacterial hand sanitizer
- ☐ Wet wipes
- ☐ Spray cleaner and paper towels
- ☐ Hand vacuum
- ☐ Duct tape
- ☐ Scissors
- ☐ Universal screwdriver
- ☐ Pliers
- ☐ Box cutter
- ☐ 3-to-2-prong plug converter
- ☐ Extra lightbulbs
- ☐ Batteries
- ☐ Extension cords
- ☐ Power strip
- ☐ Flashlight
- ☐ Plastic bags with zip closures
- ☐ Other:

Personal Items

- ☐ Small first aid kit

TAKE WITH YOU:

- ☐ Lead forms or trade show notebooks
- ☐ Orders/Action item notes
- ☐ Copies of return-shipping forms
- ☐ Filled-in appointment book/calendar
- ☐ Show management phone numbers

Trade Show Timeline

Preparing for a trade show takes organization and careful planning. One of the best ways to get a handle on everything you need to do is to set—and follow—a timeline.

9 months to 1 year before the show

- Determine your overall exhibition goals (see Step 1).
- Select the show(s) where you want to exhibit (see Step 1).
- Estimate your show budget.
- Reserve your exhibit space.
- Make travel arrangements, including reservations for accommodation.
- Decide on your *specific* goals for this show (60 new leads? 100 industry contacts?).

6 to 9 months before the show

- Select your booth design company if you're buying a pre-made booth (see Step 9).
- Begin the booth design process.
- Select show services (if not included in exhibit space rental package).
- Familiarize yourself with all show rules and regulations.
- Identify potential target customers (see Step 1).

6 months before the show

- Finalize your booth design.
- Design and produce backdrop or banner stand (if not using a booth).
- Plan your pre-show promotion strategy (see Step 3).
- Decide what types of promotional materials and giveaways to take and how many you'll need.
- Order promotional materials and giveaways.
- Review show paperwork to make sure everything has been completed and submitted

2 to 3 months before the show

- Practice setting up and taking down your pre-fab booth.
- Print copies of promotional material to take to the show.
- Prepare and print your lead forms (see page 89), if using.
- Make sure everyone from your company who will be attending the show is registered.

- Set appointments with existing clients and contacts.
- Make reservations at area restaurants for client dinners.

6 weeks to 1 month before the show

- Prepare booth and other materials for shipment to the show (see Step 10).
- Confirm with show management that all necessary services have been ordered.

1 month before the show

- Ship booth and other materials to the show (if show has restrictions about when shipments can arrive, ship materials according to those rules).
- Send first pre-show promotional email (see Step 3).
- Confirm all travel arrangements.
- Confirm safe arrival of shipped materials.
- Identify copy centers, drugstores, and office supply stores near exhibit location for last-minute emergencies.

2 weeks before the show

- Send second pre-show promotional email.

1 week before the show

- Express ship any additional or overlooked material to your hotel.

1 to 2 days before the show

- Send last-minute pre-show promotional email.

Day before show

- Arrive at show location.
- Set up booth as soon as possible.
- Confirm that all ordered show services have been provided.

3 days to 1 week after the show

- Make initial follow-up contact with show leads.

Trade Show Timeline

Use this worksheet to prioritize and track your trade show tasks.

9 months to 1 year before the show

6 to 9 months before the show

6 months before the show

2 to 3 months before the show

6 weeks to 1 month before the show

1 month before the show

2 weeks before the show

1 week before the show

1 to 2 days before the show

Day before show

3 days to 1 week after the show

Trade Show Resources

Online Sources

Advertising Specialty Institute

www.asicentral.com

Information and supplier listings for promotional items. Free registration required to search for suppliers.

Center for Exhibition Industry Research (CEIR)

www.ceir.org

A leading source of trade show industry statistics and analytical information. Annual membership (which includes access to many reports and articles) is $195.

Convention Industry Council (CIC)

www.conventionindustry.org

This forum for organizations within the trade show industry offers articles and other resources, including an excellent searchable glossary.

Exhibit Auction

www.exhibitauction.com

An online marketplace for those looking to buy and sell trade show equipment, from pop-up booths to custom exhibits. The number of items being auctioned off at any given time varies widely.

Exhibit Designers and Producers Association (EDPA)

www.edpa.com

Association for companies that design, manufacture, transport, install, and service displays and exhibits for the exhibition and event industry. Lists types of booth design companies.

Exhibitor Online

www.exhibitoronline.com

Home page of industry trade publication *Exhibitor* magazine. Offers free articles on everything from show selection to budgeting.

Exhibit Surveys Inc.

www.exhibitsurveys.com

Consulting firm specializing in quantitative exhibit industry research. Offers industry articles and white papers for free.

Expo World

www.expoworld.net

Search engine that links to thousands of domestic and international trade show industry websites. Users can search events by industry or region, look for associations, and more.

Trade Show Exhibitors Association (TSEA)

www.tsea.org

Association for anyone involved in the trade show/exhibit industry. The TSEA has a 30-plus year history offering education, advocacy, and other resources for members.

Trade Show News Network (TSNN)

www.tsnn.com

Extensive database of conferences, trade shows, and other exhibit events around the world. Also includes a supplier database, articles, and other resources.

Tradeshow Week Magazine

www.tradeshowweek.com

Home page of industry trade publication *Tradeshow Week* magazine. Includes news, articles, reports (for subscribers only), a trade show directory, and more.

Books

How to Design a "Wow!" Trade Show Booth Without Spending a Fortune
Steve Miller, with Robert Sjoquist
HiKelly Productions, Inc

How to Get the Most Out of Trade Shows
Steve Miller
NTC/Contemporary Publishing Group

Powerful Exhibit Marketing
Barry Siskind
John Wiley& Sons Canada, Ltd.

Trade Show and Event Marketing
Ruth P. Stevens
Thomson Publishing

The Trade Show Reader, Vol. 1
Julia O'Connor
TST Publishing

Entrepreneurs' Sources

The Planning Shop

555 Bryant St., #180
Palo Alto, CA 94301
(650) 289-9120

www.PlanningShop.com

The Planning Shop, publisher of this book, is *the* central resource for business planning and entrepreneurial information and advice. In addition to information and tools for developing a business plan, The Planning Shop's products provide information on starting, growing, and running a business. Planning Shop products of particular interest to trade show exhibitors include:

Business Plan in a Day

The Owner's Manual for Small Business

Six-Week Start-Up

The Successful Business Plan: Secrets & Strategies

Winning Presentation in a Day

Electronic Financial Worksheets
(Excel spreadsheets)

Index

O

P

R

S

Acknowledgments

The Planning Shop would like to thank:

For their invaluable assistance as experts on a wide range of topics relating to successful trade show exhibiting:

Emily Ashby, formerly of Blue Ridge Management Group; Heidi Genoist, Senior Editor, *Tradeshow Week* magazine (www.tradeshowweek.com); Marc Goldberg, Partner and Founder of Marketech (stafftraining.com); Mollie Hart; Mike Mraz, Trade Show Strategist; Steve Schuldenfrei, President, TSEA (www.tsea.org); Skyline Exhibits; Diane M. Williams, independent meeting/event planner, Homineata.

Rhonda Abrams would like to thank:

Maggie Canon, Managing Editor. Maggie brings an outstanding background in the publishing industry to her position with The Planning Shop. She was founding editor of *InfoWorld* and numerous other technology magazines and was also managing editor of the bestselling *America 24/7* series. Maggie's energy, professionalism, and intelligence have been invaluable additions to The Planning Shop.

Mireille Majoor, Editorial Project Manager, who oversees the editorial process of this and every Planning Shop book. She is a consummate professional and both The Planning Shop's books and readers have benefited from Mireille's commitment to excellence.

Deborah Kaye, who manages The Planning Shop's relations with the academic community. Deborah's unwavering dedication to the professors and students who use our books and resources has earned her a large group of devoted academic fans. Deborah has been The Planning Shop's guiding light for many years and we are continually appreciative of her contribution.

Rosa Whitten, Office Manager and the newest member of The Planning Shop's team. Rosa comes to us with years of organizational experience. She is already proving to be invaluable—in terms of both her skills and her positive outlook. We are delighted to have her help to guide us.

Arthur Wait, who designed the look and feel of The Planning Shop's line of books and products and developed our website and electronic products. We are always amazed (though no longer surprised) by the range of Arthur's talents.

Diana Van Winkle, who brought her graphic expertise to the design of this book. She is talented, responsive, and a delight to work with. Diana's skills ensure that The Planning Shop's books continue to be easy and pleasurable for readers to use.

Kathryn Dean, who brought her eagle eye to the copyediting and proofing process, ensuring that our books are pristine and error free.

Betsy Bozdech would like to thank:

Pete, for being endlessly supportive and encouraging when I needed that little bit of extra motivation to stay on deadline—and for the shoulder rubs that kept me going; our cats, Clara and Badger, for keeping me company and doing their best *not* to step or shed on the keyboard; Jenn, for taking a genuine interest in my progress reports; my parents, Fran and Marek, for their constant role as my sounding board; and Mollie, for getting BabyCenter to send me with her to my first trade show so long ago.

There's more where this book came from!

Ask your bookseller about these other In A Day titles from The Planning Shop, or buy direct at:
www.PlanningShop.com

"Let me take a look at your business plan." If you've heard these words from a potential lender, investor or business partner, and you need a plan fast, this book is for you. The step-by-step guide delivers the critical, time-tested information and tools you need to develop a winning plan—quickly and efficiently.

When you've got to wow an audience—whether it's making a persuasive sales presentation to a key customer, an internal report to senior management, or a motivational keynote to a packed auditorium—this book will help you get prepped, pumped, and ready to go—fast.

Grow Your Business with The Planning Shop!

We offer a full complement of books and tools to help you build your business ***successfully***.

Ask your bookseller about these titles or visit www.PlanningShop.com